Second Thoughts on Work

Sar A. Levitan
and
Clifford M. Johnson

Center for Social Policy Studies
The George Washington University

The W. E. Upjohn Institute for Employment Research

Library of Congress Cataloging in Publication Data
Levitan, Sar A.
  Second thoughts on work.

  Rev. ed of: Work is here to stay, alas. c1973.   Bibliography: p.
  Includes index.
  1. Labor and laboring classes—United States—
1970-   .   2. Work.   I. Johnson, Clifford M.
II. Title.
HD8072.5.L48   1982   331.11'0973   82-13532
ISBN 0-88099-000-7
ISBN 0-88099-001-5 (pbk.)

Graphics by **Al Lediard,** *Bailey Montague & Associates*

Foreword

The nature of work and the composition and expectations of the workforce have undergone considerable change in recent years. Numerous observers of emerging trends in occupational structure and labor force participation have predicted crises such as the mass displacement of workers by technology or the deterioration of the work ethic in American society. Levitan and Johnson challenge such views with an analysis based heavily on statistical evidence of labor market trends and conditions.

Tracing the broader evolution of work in America, the authors note the positive and gradual nature of many of the changes which are reshaping the nature of work today. However, they also acknowledge labor market problems which stem from uneven distribution of societal gains. SECOND THOUGHTS ON WORK provides a perspective for better understanding the history and contemporary reality of work, and for identifying issues and problems which will require public policy attention in the years ahead.

Facts and observations presented in this study are the sole responsibility of the authors. Their viewpoints do not necessarily represent the positions of The W. E. Upjohn Institute for Employment Research.

E. Earl Wright
Director

Labor Day, 1982

The Authors

SAR A. LEVITAN is Research Professor of Economics and director of the Center for Social Policy Studies at The George Washington University. He has been a consultant to various governmental agencies and has served on labor panels for the Federal Mediation and Conciliation Service and the American Arbitration Association. Included among the many books he has authored or coauthored are *Federal Aid to Depressed Areas; Programs in Aid of the Poor for the 1980s; The Great Society's Poor Law; Human Resources and Labor Markets; The Promise of Greatness; Shorter Hours, Shorter Weeks: Spreading the Work to Reduce Unemployment; Warriors at Work; The Volunteer Armed Force; More Than Subsistence: Minimum Wages for the Working Poor;* and *Evaluating Federal Social Programs: An Uncertain Art.*

CLIFFORD M. JOHNSON is a research associate at the Center for Social Policy Studies at The George Washington University and a former Congressional Aide. He is a graduate of Princeton University.

Preface

Every generation selects new problems, real or imagined, on which to focus its energies. Whether influenced by changing perceptions of reality or impatience with the slow pace of change, society's agenda is forever being revised. Old problems quickly give way to new issues "discovered" by reporters in search of a story, by academics in search of a reputation, or by politicians in search of a platform. Even when basic social and economic conditions evolve slowly and predictably, the spotlight of public concern seldom rests for long on a single subject.

Our perceptions of the nature of work offer no exception to this pattern. Since Adam was banished from the Garden of Eden, the debate over work has persisted, but with ever-changing emphases. In the 1960s, national attention focused on poverty and labor market analysts worried about the ability of a changing economy to provide jobs for all persons seeking employment. At the end of that decade, even though the evils of poverty and unemployment had not disappeared, the attention of many policymakers and social scientists moved on to the design of jobs and the plight of blue-collar workers. As the 1970s continued, this concern for the quality of work broadened to include a diverse array of work reform experiments, culminating in the current interest in worker participation and innovative management techniques. There is little reason to believe that the socioeconomic forces shaping the nature of work have fluctuated dramatically during the last twenty years, and yet students of the labor market have always managed to highlight something new and different.

SECOND THOUGHTS ON WORK is an attempt to transcend the narrow scope of such periodic shifts in focus and to trace the broader evolution of work in America. In examining what is happening at today's workplace and what work will be like in the future, the analysis relies heavily upon statistical evidence of labor market trends and conditions. The wealth of data collected by governments and researchers is not without limitations, but these sources can be used to gauge the relative strength of contemporary claims regarding the future of work. Contrary to predictions of imminent crisis, the evidence reminds us that work's many functions and roles ensure a more gradual pace of evolutionary change.

In writing about the future of work, it is impossible to avoid the question of semantics: What is "work"? In common usage, the word refers to a myriad of activities—artists work on paintings, pensioners work in their gardens, volunteers work without pay. Usually, the term "work" is used as shorthand for activities through which we earn a livelihood, but this definition is necessarily arbitrary. The professional athlete who earns his living by playing tennis works, but the amateur who relaxes after work with a set of tennis is playing. The housewife who tends to her own family's needs is not working, but if she is paid to labor in someone else's home she is working. A "workaholic" may toil more for pleasure than for money, but the financial compensation makes it work nonetheless.

Yet work has always conjured up other feelings and implications as well. For most of us, the term refers to activities which we feel compelled to do rather than those which we would freely choose if left to our own devices. Historically, work has also been closely associated with society's collective survival, although in an era in which a minority of the workforce produces more than enough for our sustenance this connotation is becoming antiquated. As an alternative, much of our "work" is best described as sustained and purposeful activity to accomplish goals, the continuing struggle to bend the world to our will and imagination. In this form, work provides us with a sense of community, purpose and identity, and plays an integral part in shaping life's meaning.

Despite this ambivalence toward work, Americans show no sign of abandoning the labor market. To the contrary, the evidence suggests that many of the changes which are reshaping the nature of work today are positive—generating increased options with regard to work and broadening opportunities for leisure. Disturbing trends in the workplace remain, but they stem more from the uneven distribution of societal gains than from any deterioration of work quality or job satisfaction. Hopefully, this book will serve as a reminder of our many blessings, while at the same time identifying those problems which truly warrant our greatest energies in the years ahead.

As a revision to *Work Is Here To Stay, Alas,* prepared with William Johnston, this book offered an opportunity not only to revise the data but also to test earlier judgments. Even as many trends identified in the 1973 version of the book continued throughout the decade, other developments required more detailed consideration in this revision. The dramatic gains achieved in the use of computerized technologies and the surge of interest in participative management techniques in the late 1970s have received specific attention in this regard. The revision also provided a chance to refine arguments presented in the earlier edition, so that more careful distinctions have been made between work motivation and participation in the labor force, and more detailed analyses are offered in discussing the tensions inherent in work reform efforts. Finally, this sequel includes some brief remarks on the challenges for public policy implicit in current trends in work.

Although William Johnston has gone on to other endeavors and consequently did not participate in the revision, many of his insights into the nature of work and his contributions to the earlier book have withstood the test of time and are retained in the present work. In addition, the publication of this revision was greatly facilitated by the contributions to an earlier draft of Steve Silberman, for which we are most grateful. We are also indebted to Jack Barbash and Rick Belous for helpful critical comments. The art work enlivening the prose was prepared by Al Lediard of Bailey Montague & Associates, while Nancy Kiefer went through the various drafts preparing the book for publication.

SECOND THOUGHTS ON WORK was prepared under a grant from the Ford Foundation to the George Washington University's Center for Social Policy Studies. In accordance with the Foundation's practice, responsibility for the content was left completely to the authors.

Sar A. Levitan
Clifford M. Johnson

Labor Day, 1982

Contents

1 Changes at Work

Life grants nothing to us
mortals without hard work.

—Horace, *Satires*

As the cornerstone of civilized society, there was little reason in centuries past to question either the nature or the future of work. From Biblical times well into the 20th century, work was intimately linked to both individual and collective survival, a necessity of life which required no explanation. Occasionally an author paused to examine the hardships of common laborers, but never with the expectation that their lot could be changed. Even if a handful were fortunate enough to enjoy a life of leisure, the prospect of a society in which many individuals were freed from work was beyond imagination for all but the most recent generations.

When earlier writers did turn their attention to the institution of work, it was usually in fear of some dwindling commitment to work which might threaten national survival and progress. As Sigmund Freud suggested, "After primal man had discovered that it lay in his own hands, literally, to improve his lot on earth by working, it cannot have been a matter of indifference whether another man worked."[1] Thus, in both religious and secular literature the virtues of dedication and hard work were repeatedly extolled. In early American history, these themes are easily traced—Benjamin Franklin lamented that working days were being wasted "expensively at the ale house," and nearly a century later Abraham Lincoln still viewed the desire to work as "so rare a want that it should be encouraged." These comments reflected popular views of prior generations, in which the nation was portrayed as teetering on the brink of economic and moral decline due to a widespread aversion to work.

The unprecedented economic growth and affluence during the three decades following World War II has begun to alter the way we view work in modern societies. In many ways, work no longer has the obvious role or significance which it carried for our predecessors, if only because each individual's labor is no longer essential for societal or even personal sustenance. All but a tiny part of the workforce in 1900 was working to produce the goods necessary for common survival, but now more than six of every ten workers have no hand in these activities. We now have more cosmetologists than plumbers, more social workers than brickmasons, and more professors than coal miners. Our range of work options is broader than ever before, and at least collectively we have been freed from the constant struggle for survival. In this sense, work increasingly represents our will rather than our curse.

Modern Fears and Hopes

As we move ever further away from the direct production of goods, the option of changing work—or abandoning it completely—becomes more significant. Inevitably, it seems less clear why we work, and so the traditional fears of a decadent society that values leisure more than work persist. Yet in a more optimistic vein, this new freedom makes us wonder how our jobs might be reshaped in response to more lofty goals and needs. Thus, for perhaps the first time, we have become concerned not only with our motivation or willingness to work but also with our satisfaction at the workplace.

Those who perceive work as integrally related to social stability continue to view the weakening ties between work and survival with alarm. For example, David Riesman argued that the expansion of leisure "threatens to push work itself closer to the fringes of consciousness and significance."[2] Daniel Bell views current trends in leisure and affluence as undermining the Protestant work ethic,[3] and Christopher Lasch also contends that Americans identify "not with the work ethic but with the ethic of leisure, hedonism, and self-fulfillment."[4] Such predictions of work's demise are seldom dispassionate—more typical is Arthur Schlesinger's warning that "the most dangerous threat hanging over American society is the threat of leisure."[5] The fear of a decaying work ethic is so pervasive that the federal Department of Commerce initiated in the 1970s an advertising campaign to bolster an allegedly weakening commitment to work.

Of course, even if one accepts the premise that the will to work is eroding, the vision of the future which follows depends largely on one's view of human nature. Utopian forecasters rely on the same presumed trend toward a workless society which prophets of doom project, but these more optimistic observers view leisure as a stimulus rather than a threat to societal advancement. For those who see leisure as enhancing human development, technology becomes a panacea which frees individuals from the necessity of work without sacrificing gains in economic well-being. One may question the underlying view of a world without work, but such an eventuality would no doubt offer opportunities as well as dangers.

Analysts of work quality and worker satisfaction usually do not stretch recent gains in leisure into projections of a workless society, but they are often guilty of other excesses. In contrast to the image of technology as the great liberator from work, technological change is frequently portrayed as necessarily eliminating skilled work roles and reducing prospects for personal satisfaction at the workplace. Claims of widespread discontent among workers are forcefully advanced, along with sweeping promises of newly designed jobs which would heighten satisfaction within the workforce. In the eyes of work reform advocates, modern workers seek a wide array of challenges and rewards in their jobs, and employers have considerable latitude in redesigning jobs to meet these emerging needs. It is an appealingly optimistic vision, but one that may overestimate both our character and our capabilities.

When viewed collectively, contemporary discussions of work motivation and satisfaction present widely divergent visions of work's future, ranging from the catastrophic to the utopian. These disparate accounts reflect the ample room for confusion created by rapid changes in labor force participation, occupational structure, and technology during the past few decades. Particularly when based on isolated trends, most sketches depicting the future of work shed more light on the hopes and fears of their authors than on the nature of tomorrow's workplace. Yet when labor market data are carefully examined in the context of broader social changes and market forces, a more coherent view of work in the 1990s and beyond emerges.

Chasing Expectations

The broad outlines of work's future will be shaped by the level of our expectations at the workplace and by our relative ability to respond to them. Although their influence reaches far beyond the labor market, current trends in wealth, education, and technology provide the driving forces behind the gradual evolution of work, raising expectations and setting the limits within which we can hope to fulfill them. Because of their scope, these sweeping changes in American society are frequently overlooked or given scant attention in topical studies of the workplace. Yet it is this set of forces which will have the greatest role in defining the goals of tomorrow's worker, affecting both the motivation to work and the prospects for job satisfaction.

The most pervasive force behind rising expectations is the increasing wealth of American society. The trend toward affluence is unmistakable: in the last three decades, the average American's spendable income has risen 87 percent, after allowing for inflation and higher federal income and payroll taxes. Thirty-five percent of all families had an income of $25,000 or better in 1979, compared to only 8 percent with real incomes that high a quarter of a century earlier. Cast in more vivid terms, Americans spent more on liquor alone in 1981 than their grandparents and great-grandparents did on all goods and services a century ago. This unprecedented growth in real incomes has radically revised our lifestyles, but more importantly it has lowered our tolerance for hardship and led us to expect even further gains.

To the extent that economic necessity provides a prime motivation to work, increasing affluence has weakened the ties between workers and their jobs. In addition to swelling the ranks of the independently wealthy, rising incomes have made possible a host of transfer payments which give many others the option not to work. During the 1970s, a decade commonly associated with conservative climates, these transfer payments increased 77 percent in real terms—an expansion of the welfare state without parallel. Most of these payments went to the retired, disabled and unemployed workers, and veterans, with less than one-fifth of the total devoted to "public assistance" provided on the basis of need. While the great majority of Americans still find it necessary to work, the evolution of the welfare state has softened the consequences of not working and provided new choices (such as early retirement) to those who do work.

The rising incomes and expectations of recent decades have had a mixed impact on work motivation. As burgeoning transfer payments approach one-sixth of the nation's disposable income, and assuming real earnings resume their dominant upward course, Americans increasingly will be able to change jobs or reject work in response to rising expectations. At the same time, however, relative income appears to be much more relevant to work motivation than any absolute gains, so that individuals have strong incentives to keep working no matter what release from work they could have collectively reaped from productivity gains. Like the mechanical rabbit leading the greyhounds around the racetrack, goals have consistently stayed ahead of productivity. This alone will keep most of us tied to work in the decades ahead.

In the same manner that rising affluence has led us to expect steadily growing incomes, rising levels of educational attainment have caused us to expect greater challenges and skill requirements in our jobs. Again, the data reflect unquestionable gains in education: In the three decades following 1950, the proportion of the adult population that completed four years of high school almost doubled, jumping from 34.3 percent to 67 percent. Half of American workers had at least a whiff of college education (12.7 years of schooling) by 1980, four more years than attained by the average worker in 1940 when half the labor force had barely completed elementary school. In virtually all occupational categories, Americans are entering the labor force later and with more educational background than ever before, creating both opportunities and strains at the modern workplace.

If a few added years of history and algebra represented the full scope of educational expansion, the impact on worker expectations might be rather limited. Yet these extensions of formal education have been accentuated by a veritable "information explosion" which has raised the gazes of even the most isolated Americans far beyond their immediate surroundings. Unlike the closed world of our grandparents—without radio, television, and often even newspapers—in which values and aspirations changed slowly, we are now more aware of the lives which others enjoy. With this greater awareness, "overeducated" workers are more likely to be unhappy in their jobs or even to reject the work which society requires for its maintenance. The educational gains do create the possibility of more demanding work roles, but the failure of skill requirements to keep pace with educational improvements is likely to leave workers less, rather than more, satisfied with their jobs.

Finally, as changes in relative wealth and access to information raise expectations, changes in technology will dictate the extent to which we can respond to new demands at the workplace. Technological advances have broadened occupational choices for some, freeing women from housekeeping chores and transforming the world into a much smaller place through innovations in transportation and communications. For other segments of the workforce, technological change is a more ominous force, eliminating skilled jobs and displacing workers in declining manufacturing industries. The development of new technologies does not lead in a single direction in the formation of tomorrow's workplace, but it does present a set of real constraints too often overlooked by those who would reshape work to meet rising expectations.

Any one of these broad social changes, when viewed in isolation, can be used as the basis for extreme predictions regarding the future of work. Increasing wealth has been linked to both the demise of work and as the key to expanding occupational choice and worker satisfaction. Added education and greater awareness lead some to project revolutions at the workplace while causing others to hope for an era of increasingly skilled and challenging work roles. Technology may render workers obsolete, or simply eliminate the most harsh and unrewarding jobs while opening new work opportunities. In all areas, the changes are so broad as to create endless possibilities for their selective application, but such prophecies are myopic and misleading. Only when viewed together and assessed with the guidance of current labor market data is it possible to construct a coherent picture of the future of work in a rapidly changing society.

The Commitment to Work

The dangers of extrapolating disparate trends are most clearly demonstrated by predictions that work will disappear. Although the vision of a society in which many are freed from work is not illogical, current work patterns do not support such claims, but reflect great continuity with the work habits of our predecessors. The length of the full-time workweek, which steadily decreased during the first four decades of this century, has stabilized at a nearly universal 40-hour week since World War II. More surprisingly, the proportion of the population that works has actually increased during this century, bolstered by growing labor force participation among women. Even recent survey results confirm a continuing attachment to work—a Roper Organization survey found that only one in five people place more emphasis on their personal satisfaction and pleasure than on working hard and doing a good job,[6] and 85 percent of those interviewed by the American Council of Life Insurance believe that success in life is dependent on their working hard.[7] If we are really about to abandon work, somebody had better tell the workers.

Rising levels of affluence among American workers have had an effect on work trends—today's jobholders are increasingly opting for greater leisure through paid vacations and holidays, and they are also spending fewer years of their lives working than ever before, retiring earlier in spite of growing life spans. Yet any expectations of freedom from work have been matched by expectations of higher incomes, limiting the scope of movements away from work. Rather than shunning their jobs, Americans have responded to rising productivity and affluence partially by seeking higher incomes and partially by enjoying more "free time" while employed. These choices reflect somewhat predictable market decisions regarding the marginal utility of additional income and leisure, and such work-leisure tradeoffs can be expected to continue in the years ahead.

The economic incentives to work will not dissipate for the great majority of workers in the foreseeable future, and even this unlikely event would not lead to a workless society. Work fulfills a variety of needs in modern societies, providing not only an income but a sense of identity, of community and of purpose. Already we call many activities freely chosen by individuals "work," and as we move further away from the effort to clothe and feed ourselves, our understanding of the nature of work will continue to change. Feudal lords would probably not have viewed many of our contemporary pursuits as work, but according to a modern definition we will continue to work nonetheless.

work (wŭrk), *n.* [ME. *werk;* AS. *werc, weorc;* akin to G. *werk;* IE. base **werg̑-*, to do, act, seen also in Gr. *ergon* (for **wergon*), action, work (cf. ERG), *organon,* tool, instrument (cf. ORGAN)], 1. bodily or mental effort exerted to do or make something; purposeful activity; labor; toil. 2. employment: as, out of *work.* 3. occupation; business; trade; craft; profession: as, his *work* is selling. 4. *a*) something one is making, doing, or acting upon, especially as one's occupation or duty; task; undertaking: as, he laid out his *work. b*) the amount of this: as, a day's *work.* 5. something that has been made or done; result of effort or activity; specifically, *a*) *usually pl.* an act; deed: as, a person of good *works. b*) *pl.* collected writings: as, the *works* of Whitman. *c*) *pl.* engineering structures, as bridges, dams, docks,

Satisfaction at the Workplace

The continuing willingness of Americans to work is no guarantee of their satisfaction at the workplace. Workers may reluctantly conclude that unrewarding jobs are preferable to no jobs at all, but the potential for worker discontent remains a legitimate source of concern. At the same time, if claims of widespread dissatisfaction at the workplace are to become mandates for public or private remedies, the burden of proof must lie with the critics of work. Thus far, their case has not been convincing.

Efforts to gauge worker dissatisfaction and identify shifts in such attitudes over time pose numerous research problems. Surveys which attempt to assess worker discontent are plagued by methodological shortcomings, with results varying widely depending on how survey questions are phrased and responses collected and interpreted. Because work is so closely associated with one's identity and self-esteem, measures of work satisfaction invariably provoke defensive reactions which preserve one's self-image and dignity. Hence, workers are found to be generally satisfied with their jobs, but also to feel underutilized and inadequately challenged by their work roles. Without admitting that they have "settled" for unsatisfying jobs, respondents react to specific questions of work quality by criticizing the constraints inherent in their roles and thereby preserving their sense of self-esteem.

As difficult as it is to develop meaningful measures of worker satisfaction, it is even harder to construct defensible claims of long term changes in worker attitudes. While sizable portions of the workforce are no doubt (and justifiably) unhappy with their jobs, we have little basis for comparing this level of dissatisfaction with that of prior generations. The few available longitudinal studies on work satisfaction have encountered difficulties in distinguishing attitude changes of workers as they grow older from broader societal shifts over time. For this reason, we may believe that worker discontent is sufficiently prevalent to warrant public attention and concern, but calls for remedial action based on the claims that dissatisfaction is spreading and work quality deteriorating are sorely lacking empirical support.

Looking at the occupational shifts already underway in the labor market, it seems impossible to predict whether the prospects for satisfaction at the workplace will improve or diminish in the foreseeable future. The well-worn generalizations concerning shifts from blue-collar to white-collar and from manufacturing to service roles identify the broad directions of occupational change, but these observations reveal surprisingly little about the future quality of work. White-collar or service jobs will not necessarily be better or more rewarding than those which they replace, and much will depend on the expectations which tomorrow's workers bring to these new jobs. The most certain and significant variables in the satisfaction of future generations are the continuing gains in education and awareness among workers, which may lead to deeper concerns for work quality within the ranks of both labor and management. Revolution at the workplace still seems most unlikely, but a gradual evolution of priorities at work could have an important effect on the nature of jobs in decades to come.

The Attempt to Reform Work

Most discussions of work reform stem from a belief that much of today's work is unacceptably bleak and unrewarding. Such judgments are inherently subjective, and run the risk of underestimating the full diversity of worker interests and needs which shape expectations and attitudes on the job. Nevertheless, there remains a humanitarian quality to work reform efforts which justifies their pursuit even in the absence of impending crises. Where the potential for improving the organization and design of work exists within the bounds of technological and economic constraints, no threat of uprising should be necessary to ensure work reform initiatives.

The accumulating literature on work reform—first focusing on costly job redesign schemes and more recently on broad issues of participative management—has served a useful purpose. Advocates of work reform have succeeded in calling the attention of managers to the costs of excessive specialization and to the potential for tapping the knowledge of workers. Another byproduct of the work reform debate has been the occasional readiness of managers to reconsider the importance of worker commitment and morale as a "human variable" in analyses of production efficiency. Although the wholesale revision of work organizations has rarely been attempted, the critics of work have at least temporarily alerted some management and labor representatives to unattended problems in the workplace. The extent to which reform advocates can sustain that interest and actually change established practices remains to be seen.

Because they have tended to overstate their case, proponents of work reform are likely to encounter considerable skepticism in the years ahead. Concentrating on visions of meaningful work and rhetoric about the elimination of "dehumanizing" jobs, advocates of "work enrichment" and job redesign have failed to heed the technological constraints and economic considerations which establish the limits of potential work reform. They paid scant attention to questions of who will bear the costs of reforming work and what incentives managements will have to do so. Furthermore, specialized functions in work organizations were treated as though they were developed on a wholly irrational basis; Adam Smith's famous observations on the effect of a division of labor in the manufacture of pins are somehow forgotten.[8] Assuming that reform initiatives are designed to be implemented voluntarily in a manner consistent with market forces, their prospects for adoption seem far more limited than advocates suggest.

It is appealing to imagine a world in which there are no losers, in which both labor and management benefit by new approaches to work design and management. Under this scenario, workers would enjoy new challenges and accept greater responsibility in their jobs, heightening prospects for self-fulfillment at the workplace. Similarly, managers would be compensated for the time and effort they devoted to work reform by the increased productivity of a more satisfied workforce. Yet such anticipations assume an overriding community of interest between labor and management far different from the adversarial roles which have characterized American labor-management relations. While hard times may spur brief periods of reconciliation and cooperation between employers and their workers, such spells are not likely to be long-lived.

Redesigned jobs or participative management efforts may serve as good public relations props, but private firms cannot be expected to spend money for the sole purpose of enhancing worker satisfaction. While cooperation may be possible on narrowly-defined projects of limited duration, the commitment of management to work reform experiments will last only as long as they generate tangible returns in improved product quality and higher profits. And if workers perceive reform initiatives as giving management higher profits while they get far less tangible rewards, even labor support for such experiments may be shortlived.

Dramatic improvements in work quality—with worker satisfaction given priority over productivity and profits—will be achieved only through the traditional adversarial mechanisms of labor-management relations, won as workers' rights in the same manner as higher pay, safer working conditions, and restrictive work rules. To date, organized labor has not been willing to push work quality issues in collective bargaining, at least in part because the rank and file are not prepared to trade pay and benefits for less tangible or known rewards. As the education and expectations of workers continue to rise, however, unions may extend their agenda to include these issues, thereby ensuring a more lasting and determined move toward satisfying work in the years ahead.

The Future

In rejecting more dramatic claims of a disintegrating work ethic or of workplaces redesigned along utopian lines, the picture of the future which remains is more one of gradual change than of radical departures from work as we know it today. Americans will continue to work, although more and more will enjoy the benefits of leisure through longer vacations, added paid holidays, and more part-time employment. Menial and unrewarding jobs will persist, although the incumbents will increasingly wear a white collar or perform their work in service roles as opposed to the classic stereotypes of harsh factory work. Consultants will envision better worlds using values and priorities we all might embrace, but in the absence of sharp political and economic upheavals the technological and economic forces of the marketplace will continue to dictate the organization and design of work.

There are a number of encouraging trends to be found in current work patterns. Growing segments of the workforce will enjoy freedom of choice in work, selecting their preferred occupations and switching jobs with relative ease. Leisure gains will allow individuals unprecedented control over their lives, enabling them to pursue their interests outside of work as well as selecting the work they will do on the job. There is even some hope that the needs and motivation of workers will be given additional attention in the coming decades, as human resources are reassessed for their potential contributions to economic growth.

This relatively bright outlook of the future of work is clouded by the awareness that not all segments of the labor force will share its fruits. Amidst disturbing signs of a widening gap between the most and least fortunate workers, the danger to American society is that increasing numbers of workers will be excluded from productive work or confined to menial and unrewarding jobs. The pace of technological change threatens to displace growing numbers of workers in declining manufacturing sectors, and the expansion of skilled employment will be of little consolation to the uneducated with limited or narrow skills. The challenge for public policy in the labor market will be to minimize these disparities in work experience, and to ensure that opportunities are offered for those left behind to partake in a society of growing affluence, freedom and leisure at work.

2 The Meaning of Work

Let us be grateful to Adam,
our benefactor. He cut us
out of the 'blessing' of idleness
and won us the 'curse' of labor.

—Mark Twain

Any attempt to discern future patterns of work must begin with a clear sense of why people work. The motivation to work is hardly self-evident—some people enjoy their jobs, while others relish only the paycheck. The diversity of reactions toward work is partly attributable to objective differences in the tasks which various jobs require, but more importantly it stems from the broad range of expectations which are brought to the workplace. In a world with many happy auto mechanics and disgruntled corporate executives, there can be no hierarchy of jobs or set of personal needs and interests which is applicable to all. The forces which are woven into work motivation are much more complex and difficult to predict.

Popular wisdom usually ties work motivation to some vague notion of the "work ethic," which in the extreme describes only a willingness to work while revealing nothing about one's reasons for working. Thus, even though a poet, a preacher and a plumber would likely offer very different explanations for why they "work," we count them all as staunch supporters of the "work ethic." Conversely, when

17

we decry the disintegration of the "work ethic," we envision a world in which everyone refuses to work and civilizations crumble. It is a useful form of shorthand at times, but offers no guidance for assessments of work's future.

Discussions of work motivation are complicated by historical overtones, for our perceptions of the "work ethic" and of the desirability of work are influenced by ideas shaped over many centuries. The extent to which images from the past accurately reflect the realities of work in prior eras is not easily determined, for the writing of philosophers and theologians tell us more about intellectual and religious movements than what the Greek helots or medieval serfs thought about work motivation. Yet there are links between the evolution of ideas about work and changes in the nature of work itself, and both the perception and substance of work in earlier times still exert powerful influences on work patterns today. An understanding of the development of historical views toward work thus provides an important basis for examining contemporary sources of work motivation and satisfaction.

Early Concepts: The Curse of Adam

The earliest commentaries on the nature of work were far from positive. From the ancient philosophers into the sixteenth century, two basic concepts dominated intellectual and philosophical views on the role of work in society.[1] First, work was equated with the effort (usually physical) required to satisfy survival needs. Second, this effort was accepted not as an end in itself, but as a means by which others might be freed to pursue higher goals. Work, conceived as an unpleasant reality, could only impede the search for ultimate ends, and was to be avoided whenever possible.

The writings of the early Greek philosophers were firmly rooted in this view of work. Aristotle declared that just as the ultimate goal of war was peace, so the object of work was leisure. As an end in itself, leisure meant activity pursued free of compulsion or desire for gain—for example, music or contemplation. Aristotle saw work as a burden which he had no duty to bear, accepting slavery because it freed him for leisure and higher pursuits. The slaves left no written record of their feelings about such arrangements, and their plight seldom captured the recorded attention of those who profited by their labors.

Biblical and later Christian views of work were similar to these early Greek concepts. There was no work in the Garden of Eden. In the book of Genesis, toil was a curse imposed upon Adam and Eve as a symbol of their banishment from God. In later Christian writings, work became a necessary activity of this earthly world; yet the work of this life was supposed to be of little consequence compared to the spiritual work of preparing to face God. By itself, work had no meaning. Only the contemplation of God could redeem life.

All of these views of work had in common a hierarchical image of the world in which work and workers were low on the scale. Even the language reflected this perspective—the Hebrew word for "work," *avodah,* is derived from the same root as *eved,* meaning "slave." Work by definition included servitude and compulsion (the thought of freely choosing to work was inconceivable), and work effort engendered neither distinction nor respect. Rather than a laudable or joyful activity, work was an often unpleasant means to other ends, at best stones on the path to a better reality. Labor purified, but only in that the soul might turn itself more fully toward higher ends. Aquinas thought that the simplest, most routine tasks were best because they held no danger of distracting the mind from its higher purposes.

These early views of work and leisure were rational responses to a world of work which encompassed virtually nothing but physical labor, and which rendered the idea of "meaningful" or "challenging" work inconceivable. If Aristotle were living in the 1980s, we would almost certainly consider him to be working—as an author, a tutor, or whatever—but in his time such intellectual pursuits were antithetical to the concept of work. Leisure and work were as distinct as mind and body, with each the joy or the curse of a separate social class. Few were so fortunate as to escape work entirely; for the vast majority, there was no avoiding a harsh world of strenuous and unending labor.

Birth of the Work Ethic

It remained for the developments of the Renaissance and Reformation to relieve work of its temporary, means-to-an-end, bottom-of-the-hierarchy status. The ideas which altered this curse-of-work perspective evolved along many fronts. For example, the emergence of democratic ideas challenged the hierarchical image of the world. The long-accepted right of a few to a life of leisure was questioned, and utopian models were developed in which all shared equally in both leisure and labor. Similarly, some challenged the notion that this world was simply a dreary way station on the path to paradise. The blossoming of science and craft began to glorify and explore efforts to transform the world. Rather than waiting patiently for miracles, the Renaissance philosophers discarded the thesis that they could not presume to alter God's universe. Labor, no longer only an evil to be avoided, became an activity in which many took pride and enjoyment.

This transformation of work's image was to a large extent a secular outgrowth of technological, demographic and economic change. With the birth of modern science during the Renaissance, engineers and craftsmen began to replace abstract theorists and feudal lords as dominant actors shaping society's future. The merchant class also gained increasing influence as populations grew and cities expanded. While the privileged retained their rank, the men who sought to change existing social and economic institutions were doing so through work, and the interests of these emerging classes were dependent upon the existence of a stable and malleable labor force. Thus, work became not only a respected activity for the fortunate, but also a moral imperative for those laboring beneath them.

The Work Ethic

This emerging work ethic, spawned by secular forces, was reinforced with religious doctrine. By advancing the belief that work was good, that all men should work, and that even menial jobs were worth doing well, the Protestant church placed the imprimatur of God himself on work. Reformers such as Luther and Wesley declared that work was the individual's missionary contribution to God and the path to salvation. By proclamation, if not in fact, work was transformed from the accursed to the blessed, and labor (in this life at least) became an end in itself. Work became the rightful duty of all, and leisure (defined now as idleness) was declared to be the worst sin.

This complete reversal of recorded attitudes toward work preceded the industrial revolution and the universal education systems which are sometimes credited with spawning the work ethic. Still, the work ethic was eagerly adopted by society as a response to the needs of mass production. Because the efficiency of developing industries relied upon willing and diligent labor, every agent of authority and education proclaimed the virtues of work throughout the several hundred years following the Reformation. From Luther to Ben Franklin and Horatio Alger, workers received a steady diet of exhortation and incantation from press, pulpit, and primer. All work was laudable, work well done would inevitably bring reward, work shirked led to degradation and ruin. The idea, of course, endures both as an official caveat and as a popular idea.

The new emphasis on human capabilities among Renaissance scholars and the force of teachings stemming from religious reformers combined to grant strength and legitimacy to the idealization of work. To some extent, these revised perceptions were reinforced by changes in the nature of work itself. As the age of industrialization approached, local economies and the range of work activities became increasingly diverse, and tasks requiring considerable skills and intellectual abilities were subsumed under the definition of work. For a minority of skilled craftsmen, the intimate ties between work, physical labor and dreary exertion began to unravel, and a more equitable distribution of work gained acceptance. Yet for the masses of unskilled laborers, little changed except the setting of their servitude, and the forces of industrialization quickly made a mockery of the ideal of dignified work, although religious doctrine and secular conceptualization about the noble functions of work remained unchanged.

Industrialization and the Loss of Meaning in Work

From the first flowering of the work ethic, the religious and secular trends which gave it meaning began to disintegrate as the nature of work continued to change. While the model of the skilled craftsman did not disappear, the factory worker came to symbolize work in an industrialized society and to overshadow the considerable continuity of work in other occupational sectors. Industrialization and urbanization, the diminished authority of the church, and a gradual recognition that much of the work required by society was indeed tedious and unrewarding, all contributed to the eroding of the notion that work was a good in itself. Even if lauded in the sanctuary, work appeared once again to be the accursed obstacle standing between men and the realization of a freer, leisured paradise.

The analyses of Marx and Freud often have served as the bases for indictments of work in industrialized societies, and their writings reflected a new emphasis on sociological or psychological aspects of work. Both men argued that work plays a major role in providing individuals with a sense of purpose and significance. Marx analyzed manufacturing work in the early years of industrialization and concluded that factory labor had alienated workers from some rightful integral relation of work and meaning. Similarly, Freud held that work was the single most important factor in the psychology of self-esteem, and the central activity by which individuals gave meaning to their lives. Even though images of work in a preindustrial age—characterized by life on the farm and the craft method of manufacture—suffered from idealization, the contrasts drawn by Marx, Freud and their successors highlighted very real and important changes in the way people viewed work, and in the nature of work itself.

Prior to the machine age, the farmer and the craftsman had a close identification with their work. They owned their tools and controlled the pace of their work. The gratification derived from work efforts was immediate, rendering work rather than leisure the central focus of their lives. In this context, sharp distinctions between work and leisure were incomprehensible—work was an integral part of both survival and satisfaction. With the move from the countryside to the cities and from the workshop to the factory, however, most of this sense of intimacy with and control over work was lost forever.

Critics of the modern workplace suggest that industrialization conflicted severely with the harmony between work and the individual in several ways. Many people were removed from the production of the objects by which they lived, losing the knowledge of how the goods on which they depended were made. The symbolic link between work and fulfillment of basic needs was further weakened by the introduction of currencies and other standardized terms of trade which replaced the direct exchange of goods and services. The tools and processes of production became more complex, removed and unfamiliar—the industrial worker not only did not own the tools of the trade, but also understood them imperfectly, could not repair them, and usually did not control their pace. In an unfamiliar environment, the factory worker was alienated and left with none of the feelings of competency

and security common to the farmer and the village craftsman.

In this bleak view of industrialization, the content of work
also underwent major revision. The development of methods
and scales of production which required the coordinated efforts of tens or hundreds or thousands meant that individual
desires and rhythms had to be subordinated to imposed
schedules. Labor began to be defined and measured by time
on the clock, and huge organizations removed most individuals many layers from the center of responsibility and
control. Most importantly, the industrial process, in its
search for efficiency, compressed the scope of individual
jobs to the point that almost no production-line job required
more than a tiny fraction of an individual's capabilities.
Workers lost the clearly recognizable stake in production
which they previously enjoyed, and the outlet for creative
energy was all but destroyed in many occupations.

To the extent that work in an industrial area narrowed the
potential for fulfillment through one's job, people
presumably made sharper distinctions between work and
leisure. Fewer could find reason to adhere to the "work

ethic," at least if defined as a "conviction that work is a worthwhile activity in its own right, and not merely as a means to some important end such as material comfort or wealth."[2] Unsatisfying jobs gave rise to the goal of escaping work for leisure, and reinforced the idea that work encompassed everything that was unpleasant but necessary and continuing. Self-realization was sought increasingly during leisure time, and worker demands for paid leisure and for consumer goods and services increased. As a product of the forces of industrialization which transformed the nature of work, this sharp division of life into work and leisure has been viewed as a distinctly modern phenomenon and a significant departure from the experience of prior generations.

While this description of work "dehumanized" by the industrial transition may be shopworn, it does reflect the changed status and working conditions of some occupations during the machine age. Those involved in the industrial mass manufacture of goods certainly faced new problems, as the size of organizations grew and the scope of jobs narrowed in pursuit of greater efficiency. Similar shifts were felt outside the factory as well—concepts of specialization were adapted to service industries, and the emergence of large corporations deprived many white-collar workers of a sense of control and meaning at work. These developments may not have touched the lives of even a majority of workers in the nineteenth century, but they did generate the concepts of alienating work which most of society came to accept.

Whose Work Ethic?

The more difficult issue in the history of work is not whether its nature changed, but rather whether it was perceived differently by successive generations of workers. The writings of scholars and theologians portray a series of reversals, in which work is transformed from a curse to a blessing and religious duty, and then to a dreary and alienating necessity. Yet this process of abstracting a concept of the work ethic and then plotting its rise and fall over-simplifies complex developments and masks underlying continuities. It fails to explain why men worked, or worked hard, or what they thought of their jobs. The philosophical connotations of work did change, but their relationship to actual work patterns and worker attitudes is at best uncertain.

Clearly the Reformation, the rise of crafts and the emergence of democratic ideals gave new dignity to work. No longer just the inevitable toil by which one survived, work gained recognition among the learned and privileged as the activity by which individuals and societies progress. It is less clear whether the elitists' praise of work was ever accepted by workers, or how much it actually fueled their motivation to work. Surely many artisans had always taken pride in their crafts and had no need of a church-sanctioned morality or self-serving employers' exhortations to shore up the self-esteem they derived from their work. For those in less skilled labor, necessity no doubt played a stronger role in their journeys to work than any attempts at moral indoctrination. Andrew Carnegie may have dedicated his empire to the glory of God, but the men in his employ more likely worked for gold rather than grace.

A closer look at work habits during the early stages of mass production illustrates the weakness of moral imperatives concerning work. Turnover rates before World War I were greater than in 1980, with textile and steel mills, clothing shops, machine works and early automobile plants reporting turnover as high as 100 percent. Absenteeism was also a source of serious concern—as much as 10 percent of the workforce was absent on any given day.[3] In response to turnover rates reaching 370 percent, Henry Ford hired sociologists in 1914, hoping that they would strengthen workers' commitment to sustained work. A devotion to work certainly seemed absent from typical work patterns, even as philosophical discussions of the work ethic flourished. The work ethic has always existed more in the world of scholars than of laborers, more as a concept than as a powerful motivating force keeping people at work.

Much of the anxiety concerning the strength of the work ethic in contemporary society seems to stem from an exaggerated sense of its importance to work motivation in generations past. There has never been much evidence to support Max Weber's description of man as "driving hard against the environment because of his need to prove himself before God." The Protestant ethic may have heightened the social stigma associated with not working, but the struggle for survival offered ample motivation to work for even the most irreverent of characters. With greater affluence, workers have more opportunities to voice and act upon their discontent. Now as then, the survival of work does not depend on the motivational force of an abstract work ethic.

Theories of Work Motivation

Recognizing that the rise and fall of the work ethic is linked only tenuously to work behavior and motivation, most analysts of this century have sought other explanations for our attachment to work. A variety of possibilities have been raised, most focusing on some concept of need fulfillment. Given the diversity of both work and individuals, no single concept can fully account for why people work, but the contributions of various disciplines form the basis for a relatively comprehensive portrait of work motivation in a modern era.

Perhaps the most basic theory of work motivation describes the desire to work as part of human nature. This simple view of work motivation posits the existence of a fundamental human urge to exert oneself, a drive to learn, to achieve, and to shape one's surroundings. The presence of a "work instinct" is impossible to prove, and its strength cannot be measured. Yet this perspective on work motivation does derive legitimacy from traits we commonly associate with human nature: a sense of curiosity, a responsiveness to challenge, a capacity for pursuing hopes and aspirations. Even as the debate over whether these qualities are acquired or whether they are innate continues, the desire of most to exert and achieve is difficult to dispute.

The economic explanations for work are familiar ones. Subsistence needs create pressures for work in all civilizations, and continue to fuel work motivation even in affluent welfare states. While the aggregate wealth of society may be sufficient to free substantial portions of the population from the necessity of work, distribution systems within the economy generally ensure that people work if they wish to enjoy anything more than the most meager of incomes and lifestyles. As the Industrial Workers of the World once chanted, "We go to work to get the dough to get the food to get the strength to go to work . . . ." A paycheck is no guarantee of an escape from poverty—millions of Americans earn too little for them to avoid this fate—but the economic advantages of working are almost always sufficient to give individuals powerful incentives to remain employed.

In wealthy industrialized nations, the concern for relative income gains is a far more powerful source of work motivation than any basic survival needs. Most of the "necessities of life" in America already are a reflection of cultural norms and expectations rather than of provisions for food, shelter and clothing. This process of revising expectations upward leaves the majority working for nicer homes, cars and stereos, while only an impoverished minority still struggles to place dinner on their tables. The point is not to legitimize this distribution of income, but simply to stress that even amidst considerable wealth, the lure of relative income gains provides meaningful economic incentives to work.

In themselves, these instinctual and economic views might be sufficient to explain why most people work. Still, the most intriguing (and in affluent societies perhaps the most powerful) accounts of work motivation have emerged from sociological and psychological perspectives. Arguing that work in modern societies is more than a means of subsistence or an avenue for fulfilling economic needs, sociologists have suggested that work is also essential in providing a sense of meaning, of community and self-esteem to the individual. Through work, we seek to justify our own existence, to develop a feeling of participation in a design which is grander than our personal lives. Through work, we join a community of individuals with common experiences, skills or goals. Through work, we derive feelings of competence and achievement, making contributions which enable us to believe in our own worth.

Thus, while people may not want to labor, they usually want a job. The distinction is not merely semantic—few are compelled by the sheer excitement or challenge of their work, but by having a job they can earn social acceptance. Work is "a membership card that entitles the holder to all the privileges of bountiful culture."[4] For this reason, Americans work even when it is not imperative: millions hold jobs in spite of their eligibility for welfare at comparable income levels, and labor market studies have shown repeatedly that three of four workers would continue working even if they inherited enough money to live comfortably in leisure.[5] One person who enjoyed the good fortune of inherited wealth told journalist Studs Terkel, "I have come to some conclusions after having been free economically from the necessity of work. To be occupied is essential."[6]

The impact of unemployment on the human psyche provides a dramatic illustration of the social and psychological needs which work fulfills. For those without jobs, the psychic scars can be great. The reflections of John Coleman, a labor economist who took a sabbatical from a college presidency to try his hand at manual work, are instructive; after only day of unemployment, he wrote:

> This day hit me hard. I have a secure, or reasonably secure, job to go back to. My family's bills are being paid while I'm away. I can still use my name to open doors here and there. But none of that mattered today. I felt unwanted and out of work. I wondered why people couldn't see what a valued employee I would be . . . .[7]

Deprived of a community of co-workers and unable to contribute to the support of family or society, the jobless quickly feel alienated and unproductive. The causes of this forced idleness are of secondary importance—even when wholly beyond the individual's control, the sense of dependency, of uselessness and isolation can be devastating.

Not surprisingly, research data suggest that unemployment and mental health are inversely related, with the strains of joblessness so severe as to be potentially life-threatening. M. Harvey Brenner of Johns Hopkins University has estimated that a 1 percent increase in the U.S. unemployment rate results in some 37,000 additional deaths, with more than half of those fatalities caused by increased incidences of heart attacks and other cardiovascular diseases.[8] Obviously most people denied work do not die. But unemployment has robbed them—if not of life, then of something else. "The bewilderment they often express is like that of the homeowner who returns to find rooms ransacked, valuable and beloved objects missing," Harry Maurer concludes in his oral history of the unemployed:

> The sense of violence and invasion, the feelings of fear and loss and helplessness descend with the same stunning force when a worker is deprived of work. And the loss is much greater, because work, if the longing of the unemployed is any indication, remains a fundamental human need—even in the crushing form it has increasingly assumed in the modern world. It provides not simply a livelihood, but an essential passage into the human community. It makes us less alone.[9]

Thus, the forces which lead us to the workplace are much subtler than any proscriptions and religious moralisms of the work ethic. We work because it defines our place in the world, and creates a world in which we can feel both needed and useful.

A Worker's Identity Crisis?

"Who am I? . . . I'm a —." Almost regardless of how the response is completed—whether electrician, banker or teacher—the reply will conclude with a description of the individual's job. The sociological importance of work is epitomized by the widespread practice of defining people by their work roles, and often of characterizing ourselves in the same manner. A quick glance at the obituary page of the newspaper illustrates the point: the headlines do not announce the passing of a beloved husband, mother or neighbor, but rather of a former city councilman or social studies teacher. Terkel explored this theme repeatedly in interviews with a cross section of workers: "Your work is your identity;" it "tells you who you are;" "your occupation molds your personality;" and "my work and my life have become one" were typical replies. Even when people hated their work, Terkel concluded, it remained the reference point for identity.

Again, the attitudes of the unemployed demonstrate vividly the role of work in shaping self-image. Many jobless persons feel stripped of their identity, lost in a sea of statistics and without a role to assert in a community of workers. An unemployed forty-five year old construction worker expressed his frustration:

> Right now I can't really describe myself because . . . I'm unemployed. . . . So, you see, I can't say who I am right now. . . . I guess a man's something else besides his work, isn't he? But what? I just don't know.[10]

This link between work and identity has been perceived to be so strong as to sustain work effort even in the absence of significant economic incentives to work. A 1972 federal government report concluded:

> . . . to be denied work is to be denied far more than the things that paid work buys; it is to be denied the ability to define and respect one's self.

> It is illusory to believe that if people were given sufficient funds most of them would stop working and become useless idlers.[11]

Supported by considerable research on work attachment among the poor, it seems clear that Americans of all income levels gauge their self-esteem and identity in relation to their jobs, and that these personal needs provide compelling motivations to work.

"I just introduced Mr. Indemnity Bonds to Ms. Paralegal Services."

It is important to note that the close connection between work and identity or self-esteem has had special meaning for women in American society. With dominant values still failing to acknowledge housekeeping activities as work, millions of women have been denied the recognition or status which virtually any other "job" would confer. Betty Friedan presented one of many examples of how this lack of recognition has affected women who remain at home:

> A young mother with a beautiful family, charm, talent and brains is apt to dismiss her role apologetically. 'What do I do?' you hear her say. 'Why nothing, I'm just a housewife.' A good education it seems has given this paragon among women an understanding of the value of everything except her own worth.[12]

Not surprisingly, women increasingly are working for wages outside the home, with dramatic implications for the composition of the labor force and the nature of work. The record number of women who are working may not be as single-minded in their attachment to jobs as their male counterparts, but they are clearly expressing a desire to define themselves in terms other than John Smith's wife or Bill Jones's mother.

Thus, among all of the groups which might be presumed to have the weakest attachment to the labor market—the unemployed, the poor, and women who previously have not entered the labor force—work continues to play a powerful role. Some of the pressures to work indeed may stem from the remnants of the Protestant ethic, placing a stigma on those choosing not to work. Yet these negative forces could not fully account for the continuing strength of work motivation in modern society. The desire to work reaches far beyond pious exhortations, and even beyond the pressures of economic necessity. We work because it offers one certain way of participating in the world around us, of developing a shared sense of community and of building a sense of identity and self-esteem which adds meaning to our lives.

Who Really "Wants" to Work?

The list of reasons why we may "need" to work—whether psychological, economic or sociological—provides ample ways of understanding the motivation to work. Yet this discussion should not evoke images of workers springing cheerfully from their beds each morning, eager to reach their jobs. Just as work satisfaction is distinct from work motivation, *wanting* to work is quite different from *needing* to work. A fortunate few manage to hold jobs which they find challenging and exciting, but they are truly blessed. The struggle to cope with tedious and unpleasant work is far more common. Even if Americans do not shirk work in the coming decades, they may not rush to embrace it either.

It is perhaps most accurate to view people as of two minds, fundamentally ambivalent in their attitudes toward work. "The desire to work . . . is a powerful human need, an ego drive related to self-expression, power, creativity," concluded historian John Garraty, and yet "so . . . is the desire to be idle and free of responsibility."[13] Freud articulated the same paradox fifty years earlier, suggesting that people depend on work and yet neither prize it as a path to happiness nor pursue it as a source of satisfaction, often working only under the stress of necessity.[14] In the words of Eli Ginzberg, this "natural aversion to work" stems from the desire of workers to be "masters of their souls for as much of the day as possible."[15]

Of course, these competing desires for freedom and social recognition, for pleasure and achievement, are not new additions to human nature. Yet the fundamental human ambivalence toward work may take on increasing importance in labor markets of the future as workers gain the ability to make more personalized choices between work and leisure. In pragmatic terms, work will remain an economic necessity for all but the very rich, and the noneconomic functions of work will ensure some attachment to work throughout society. Yet workers already are gaining the option to balance work and leisure time amidst growing affluence, and these work-leisure tradeoffs reflect their ambivalence toward work. The continuing motivation to work may not disappear, but workers are increasingly able to act on their own mixed emotions toward their labors.

3 The Survival of Work

I don't like work—no man
does—but I like what is in
work—the chance to find
yourself. Your own reality—
for yourself, not for
others—what no other
man can ever know.

—Joseph Conrad
Heart of Darkness

If the demise of the work ethic is a threat to civilization, one would never suspect it from current labor market trends. Whatever their ambivalence, Americans are working more than ever. Productivity gains and growing affluence have not triggered a mass exodus from work and our society has not decayed from idleness and sloth. Instead, both greater numbers and larger proportions of the population have entered the labor force in recent years, and the tenacious hold of work upon the daily activities of most Americans shows few signs of weakening.

The Growing Labor Force

Rather than abandoning work, Americans have sought it in unprecedented numbers. The U.S. labor force has more than tripled in size since the turn of the century, and even the relative percentage of the population which works has crept up since World War II (Figure 3.1). The growing ratio of

37

38

Figure 3.1 Labor Force Participation Has Increased During the Twentieth Century

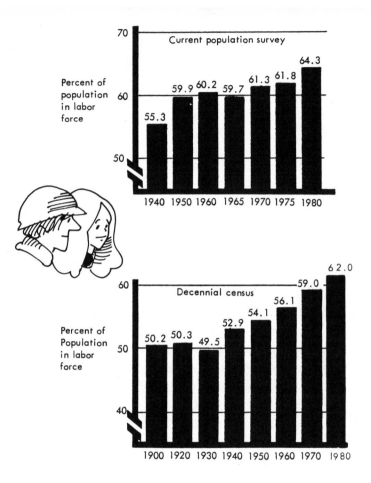

Source: U.S. Bureau of the Census, Historical Statistics of the United States, *Colonial Times to 1970* (Washington: U.S. Government Printing Office, 1975), p. 127; and U.S. Bureau of the Census, "Provisional Estimate of Social Economic and Housing Characteristics," 1982.

workers to the working age population is particularly significant when viewed in light of gains in productivity. Despite an enormous decrease in the amount of human labor required to produce given quantities of goods, no corresponding decrease in the number or relative portion of workers has taken place. Driven by rising expectations and an interest in relative income gains, individuals have continued their work effort and sought to maintain their share of society's increasing wealth.

The improvements in standards of living made possible by rising productivity are simply astounding. At the turn of the century, electric lighting and indoor plumbing were luxuries in private homes reserved for the affluent. Today, housing which lacks these "basics" is considered unfit for habitation. In 1900, food which was not locally in season could rarely be obtained, even by the wealthy. Now, even the poor routinely consume meats, fruits, and vegetables shipped from across a continent and beyond. This dramatic shift in contemporary expectations reflects the affluence of American society—in 1981, the *average* net worth per person was nearly $40,000, representing a collection of cars, TV sets, bank accounts, and real estate undreamed of even a few decades ago.

Workers have responded to the potential freedoms of rising productivity and affluence, but not in the manner feared by some. Instead of abandoning work, workers have opted for greater amounts of paid leisure to complement their rising incomes in traditional 40-hour per week jobs. Factories have not stood idle, but employers have been faced with demands for more paid holidays and longer vacations as part of the "fringe benefits" of employment. The process is one of gradual evolution, in which individuals continually adjust to rising standards of living and balance further income gains against the utility of additional "free time" away from the workplace.

Unfortunately, all segments of the population have not shared equally in either the growing affluence or the stable labor force participation which aggregate data reflect. The overall trends in labor force participation disguise significant changes in the demographic characteristics of the workforce, failing to indicate who is entering the labor force and why. A review of the participation rates of various subgroups within the labor force highlights these more detailed aspects of work motivation, and provides a firmer basis for conclusions about the future of work in contemporary America.

The Arrival of Women at Work

The increasing number of people who work each day are a new breed, or at least a distinctly more feminine one. At the turn of the century, the vast majority of workers were men. In the social order of that day, the man was the breadwinner, and the woman was the homemaker. Eighty years later, the distribution of labor between the sexes has changed radically—women have joined men at the workplace in record numbers, more than doubling their share in the labor force since 1900 (Figure 3.2). In more than 60 percent of all marriages today, the husband is not the sole provider for his family. For the first time in history, working wives out-number housewives.

The movement of women into the labor force was not a sudden revolution, but rather a "subtle revolution" which began before World War II. The workplace had long been the natural habitat for many minority and unmarried women—according to the 1900 census, 41 percent of all non-white women and 17 percent of white women (many of whom were immigrants) worked. Seventy-five percent of the female factory workers were of immigrant stock and close to 70 percent of the working women were unmarried at the turn of the century.[1] Nearly one in every five workers was female, rendering the concept of the working woman at least familiar to industrial America.

Figure 3.2   In 1981, Women Comprise More Than Twice as Large a Share of the Labor Force as in 1900

Source: U.S. Bureau of Labor Statistics.

World War II was a watershed: the social fetters which barred married, middle-class women from working were shattered by the need to replace some 12 million men who left the labor force for battle. By V-E day, 36 percent of the women of working age were employed, compared to 25 percent before the war. Within 2 years after the war, some women left the workforce, reducing labor force participation to 32 percent. Since, female labor force participation resumed an uninterrupted upward climb. Unlike the young, single, and poor women who worked in the first four decades of the twentieth century, the women who replaced the male combatants during the war were frequently married and over thirty-five years of age. Dependent upon female labor, the wartime economy legitimized the employment of married, middle-class women and triggered a pattern of increasing participation which continues to this day.

Having discovered the workplace, increasing numbers of women found that full-time homemaking had lost its attraction, despite the jump in the birth rate during the postwar period. Throughout the 1950s, new women entrants into the labor force exceeded the number of additional males, so that by 1960 nearly twice as many women were working than had been in 1940. Initially, the rush into the labor market was among mature women: 80 percent of the women entering the labor force from 1945 to 1965 were over 35 years old. Since then, the reverse has been the case—almost the same percentage of new entrants have been less than thirty-five years of age. Yet regardless of age variations, the surge of women into the work force has been unmistakable. In 1981, slightly more than 50 percent of all wives held paying jobs outside the home, compared to only 23 percent in 1947.

Why have women rushed with such vigor into the labor force in the course of just a few decades? Some social scientists turn to changing technology—in the bedroom as well as the kitchen—in their attempts to explain the labor market behavior of women. Housekeeping consumes less time today than a few decades ago and the number of children in the home has also declined, leaving more time for work. In addition, a woman now can virtually determine the number of children she will have and when she will have them. As a result of this increasing control, the average number of children per family dropped from 2.3 to 1.9 during the 1970s, with the fertility rate reaching a historic low of 15.3 births per thousand people by 1980.

Undoubtedly these technological advances have enhanced the ability of women to shape their own lifestyles, eliminating some of the burdens and uncertainties which complicated their labor force participation in previous eras. Yet changes in technology were as much a response to emerging values and demands as they were a cause of these new work patterns. Technological innovations may have facilitated female labor force participation but the opportunity to work is not synonymous with the desire to work, and a more complete explanation is needed.

Traditional economic incentives can also account only partially for the growing labor force participation of women. For some women, economic needs do play a significant role in stimulating work effort—in the aggregate, white wives account for one-quarter of their family income and black wives provide one-third of family income. Without this work effort, many Americans families could not maintain their middle-class status. Yet the strong inverse relationship between a husband's income and the labor force activity of his wife which once dominated women's work roles has weakened considerably amidst growing affluence. The Bureau of the Census reported that almost 60 percent of the women in families with annual incomes of $25,000 or more worked in 1980. According to the 1980 Virginia Slims American Women's Opinion Poll, less than 50 percent of working women took their jobs to support themselves or their families.[2] For most women, only the pursuit of relative income gains provides an economic incentive for working. Many families simply are unwilling to settle for the standard of living their parents enjoyed in the 1950s, and so women continue to enter the labor market.

The rapid movement of women into the workforce has achieved its strength and permanence due to the same sociological needs for a sense of community, identity and self-esteem which drive the work efforts of men in an affluent society. Some women no doubt always envied the work roles and related social status of their male counterparts, but until the past few decades they have had little chance to express such yearnings. The precedent of wartime labor provided the first crack in social mores which had kept women at home, and the more recent women's movement of the 1970s has ensured the steady disintegration of these rigid stereotypes. Once unleashed by social and economic change, the latent desires of women for recognition outside the home have fueled their rapid rise in labor force participation. In this sense, their motives for working remain quite similar to those of men—they just have been prevented from acting on them in earlier times.

Finally, it is important to note that this massive surge in the labor force participation of women would have been impossible in the absence of favorable labor market conditions.

Structural changes in the economy which increased the demand for female labor had enticed women into the labor force even before the women's movement flourished, and the ever-increasing participation of women has been facilitated by the growing labor requirements of an expanding economy. The rapid growth of the service sector has been particularly significant in this regard, since women traditionally performed much of the work now found in service industries. Without this demand for female labor, the "emancipation" of women from the home would have proceeded at a much slower pace. Now, given our dependence on female labor to meet current labor needs, any wholesale return to the home is inconceivable.

Men—Working but Retiring

The dramatic influx of women into the labor force has hidden a divergent trend—men are leaving the workforce with greater frequency than ever before. Since 1951, the labor force participation rate of men dropped almost continuously from 87.3 percent of the working age population to 77.5 percent three decades later. In that same period, three of every five added workers were female, and the average number of years worked in a man's lifetime steadily declined. The aggregate data are deceiving, for the expanding work effort of women has totally offset the drop in male labor force participation to produce slightly increasing overall rates. Even among men, the 11 percent decline in participation since 1951 fails to reveal sharper retreats from the labor force by older men.

While the data on male labor force participation might be used superficially to argue that work motivation indeed is disappearing, a closer examination suggests otherwise. The vast majority of able-bodied men are working as much as their fathers and grandfathers did. Even young males, who have little attachment to the workplace, have not shunned work. Only two distinct groups within the male labor force have left the workplace with increasing frequency: white men over age 55 and blacks. As with women's rising labor force participation, both these trends have been driving forces unique to these segments of the population.

Most predictions of the disintegration of work stress the absence of traditional workforce attachments among the young, and yet the labor force participation rates of American youth certainly reflect no crisis at the workplace. Although more males aged 14-24 are enrolled in school than were a generation ago, they are also working more than students did in 1955—in part because more children from less affluent families are attending college, which they finance by working. This is not to suggest that participation rates among young males have not fluctuated over time—in the mid-1960s, the rates for males aged 16-19 dipped sharply, only to rebound to approximately their 1950 levels by 1981. Coupled with the steady rise of teenage female participation over the course of the past three decades, the evidence reflects no abandonment of work at the lower end of the age spectrum.

Rather than rebellious youth, it is their older counterparts who are working less. Males forty years their junior are not postponing their entrance into the labor force, but older men are hastening the age at which they leave work. In the 1950s, nearly nine of ten men aged 55 to 64 worked. Thirty years later, less than three in four did. The drop is even more precipitous for men 65 years of age and over—from 48 percent in 1947 to 18 percent in 1981, a 61 percent decline. This weakened attachment to the labor force in later years is unique to men as well. From 1947 to 1980, the proportion of women aged 55 to 64 in the labor force jumped from 24 percent to 42 percent, while the labor force participation rate of women over 65 years of age remained unchanged. Clearly, older men are no longer viewing work in later years as an unavoidable necessity. Working until at least age 65, once a social prescription, is turning into a social suggestion.

The length of retirement for men is growing on two fronts: men are retiring earlier at the same time their life expectancy is increasing. Today, the average male at age 65 can be expected to live another 15 years. Combined with decisions to retire at earlier ages, this greater life expectancy had led to a tripling since 1900 of the number of years the average man spends outside the labor force. Even over the past two decades, the lifetime leisure gains have been considerable—in 1960, an average of 25.7 years were spent outside the labor force, but this figure for men had jumped to 31.0 years by 1977. After age 14, the number of years men spent outside the workforce rose from 10.8 years to 14.0 years (Figure 3.3). While women's work effort has lengthened with gains in life expectancy to produce a relatively constant level of lifetime leisure throughout this century, the appetite of men for greater leisure in their later years has not yet been sated.

The movement toward earlier retirement among men is partially a reflection of changing social attitudes. Once carrying the stigma of forced idleness, retirement now has taken on a more positive aura of welcomed leisure. More importantly, however, the shift toward earlier retirement is also a response to heightened private and public "subsidization of leisure" which allows more men to afford early retirement than ever before. A recent study of determinants of planned retirement age, based on data from the longitudinal history retirement study of the Social Security Administration, found that being eligible for social security benefits increases the probability of early retirement by 11.1 percent for a typical married man and 12.4 percent for a typical single woman.[3] Eligibility for a private pension was found to provide even stronger incentives for retirement between age 62 and 65. For this reason, social security data also reveal that men who had worked in low income jobs—those least likely

48

Figure 3.3 Lifetime Leisure For Men After Age Fourteen Has Tripled

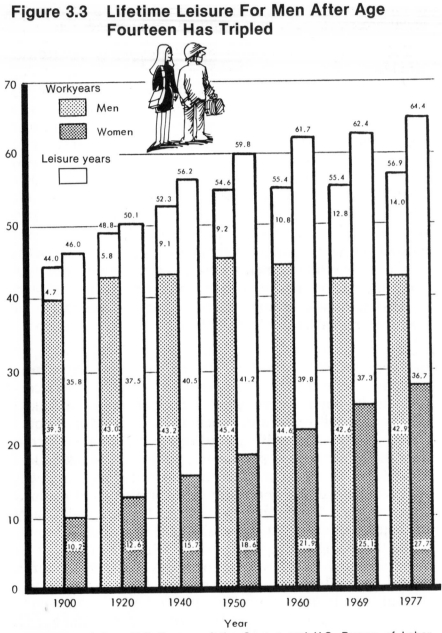

Source: Derived from U.S. Bureau of the Census and U.S. Bureau of Labor Statistics data.

to have pension coverage—were also the most likely to keep working to supplement social security benefits.[4]

The expansion of coverage and benefits under both private and public retirement systems accounts for the greater financial security which has fueled decisions to retire early. For example, the percentage of workers with private pensions more than doubled in the course of 25 years, rising from 22 percent of the labor force in 1950 to 46 percent in 1975. Similarly, the Social Security Act covered 64.5 percent of all workers thirty years ago, while in 1980 the figure was 90 percent. During the 1970s, the average monthly benefit for retired workers rose 26 percent (after adjusting for inflation), while real average weekly earnings declined by 2 percent. Finally, most pension plans—public as well as private—have lowered the age at which people may retire. More than 70 percent of all new social security recipients in 1978 were less than 65 years of age, and similar trends can be found in private retirement systems.

In essence, because "retirement" is a socially accepted departure from the labor force, older men have been able to seize the leisure gains of an affluent society in a manner impossible in earlier generations or for most workers in less productive economies. While sociological forces tie younger workers to the labor force even in the absence of economic need, older men have an "easy out" in early retirement, and thus they are one of the few groups which have responded to increasing wealth by ceasing to work. Most older men have already established their sense of identity and self-esteem through their work history, and their psychological needs for work are less pressing. For this reason, even as work continues to provide physical and mental sustenance for some, men in their later years are increasingly choosing the option of expanded leisure.

The limits to this growth of leisure through early retirement will depend on the willingness of society to subsidize the abandonment of work by older men. High inflation rates during the 1970s have severely taxed retirement systems, and benefits for retirees have grown much faster than their contributions to such systems. The problem is becoming particularly acute for public systems, including federal social security, where political pressures for expanded benefits and a "pay as you go" financing structure have combined to place the system in serious financial trouble.

In response to these concerns, shifts in government policy designed to stem the tide of early retirement are already occurring. The 1977 amendments to the Age Discrimination in Employment Act of 1967, passed ostensibly to ensure fairer treatment of older workers under age 70, may induce them to remain in the workforce longer. The ongoing debate on social security has raised the prospect of more direct efforts to discourage early retirement, including proposals advanced by the Reagan administration in 1981 to penalize persons taking advantage of early retirement (prior to age 65), to provide additional incentives for continued work efforts by beneficiaries, and to raise gradually the age of eligibility for full retirement benefits from 65 to 68. The intensity of political opposition to such changes in social security highlights the growing appeal of early retirement. Yet the willingness of the rest of society to finance ever-increasing leisure in later years still may dictate the upper limit of this powerful trend.

The Exodus of Black Men

In addition to older men, the other segment of society exiting the labor force in increasing numbers are black men. If the earlier retirement of older men is a testament to the benefits of an affluent society, the abandonment of work by black men is a sign of the failure of that same labor market to provide employment for all groups. There is some element of social progress in the declining labor force participation of blacks—younger blacks are delaying entry into the labor market in order to obtain more education, and older blacks are increasingly able to retire under expanded disability and pension coverage. Yet the overall drop in labor force participation among blacks is so precipitous that it cannot be attributed to social advance. Many black men are not leaving the labor force to embrace the joys of greater leisure; rather, their departure reflects bleak job prospects, an expression of discouragement and despair.

Disparities between the labor force participation rates of white and black men have arisen only over the past two decades. As late as 1960, the labor force participation rates of white and black men were identical—in fact, from the end of Reconstruction until the Great Depression, proportionately more blacks than whites were in the labor force. Since that time, participation rates for both whites and blacks have plummeted, but not in a similar manner. The decline among white males correlates positively with age, but for black males there is no such relationship. In all age groups, fewer blacks are now in the labor force. Falling from 85 percent in 1954 to 71 percent in 1981, this new pattern of falling work effort among black men is a source of deep concern.

The deviation of black labor force participation from that of other groups can be most consistently explained not by the presumption of structures of work motivation unique to blacks, but rather by the failure of the labor market to fulfill the needs of blacks to the extent enjoyed by other groups. Notwithstanding the progress made under the Great Society, most blacks have remained confined to demeaning, low-status jobs which promise little and deliver even less. In these work roles, black men have had little opportunity to derive a sense of identity or community through participation in the labor force, and their self-esteem often has been undermined instead of strengthened by poor job opportunities. As Elliot Liebow observes, "The streetcorner man wants to be a person in his own right, to be noticed, to be taken account of, but in this respect, as well as in meeting his money needs, his job fails him.''[5] Now ''the job and the man are even''—after having the job fail him, more black men are failing the job.

Even in strict economic terms, the labor market seldom meets the black man's needs. More than 16.3 percent of black workers had incomes below the poverty level in 1980 in spite of their employment. In this context, the withdrawal of black men from the labor force is often a sign of rationality rather than a symptom of pathology. With transfer payments frequently at least as remunerative as work, the possibility of not working becomes both a real and predictable option. Even though men are not eligible for public assistance in half the states, almost 10 percent of black males who were heads of households, as well as 25 percent of those who were not, earned no income through work. The lack of pecuniary rewards from work which fosters this welfare dependency is at best a sad commentary on the distribution of earnings and employment in America. It is not that welfare ceilings are too high—wage floors simply are too low to lift many black workers and their dependents out of poverty. Cast in this light, the willingness and motivation of blacks to work seems stronger than one might expect.

The labor market experience of black men can be explained in various ways, but the dual labor market hypothesis provides one of the most persuasive illustrations of their plight. In its most simplified form, the basic hypothesis contends that the labor market is divided into two distinct segments, one offering relatively high wages, good working conditions and job security while the other provides low paying jobs with poor working conditions and little chance for advancement. Workers trapped in secondary markets are forced to accept unstable employment, have little assurance of due process in their treatment on the job, and often work only intermittently due to lack of steady employment. The dual labor market approach contains no special theory of racial discrimination, but it deals with discrimination as one factor which influences labor market segmentation and confines many blacks to low-paying, dead-end jobs.

It is difficult to imagine a reversal of the declines in labor force participation among black men in the near future, as current developments in the labor market seem likely only to exacerbate their current plight. Labor force data strongly suggest that the incidence of unemployment is falling increasingly on already disadvantaged groups within American society, including blacks.[6] Until the labor market, most likely in response to government policies, becomes more successful in meeting the needs of black men, it should come as no surprise if growing numbers find preferable alternatives to working in legal labor markets.

Work Motivation Amidst
Poverty and Unemployment

The failure of the labor market to provide steady employment and adequate incomes has had the greatest impact on black men, but such hardship is felt throughout the population. Nearly one-half of all poor family heads and over one-third of all single poor persons in 1980 worked but were unable to earn enough to escape poverty. About one-fifth of those poor families actually had two or more persons working at some time during the year but remained poor. As of 1979, one million family heads with about four million dependents, and another 233,000 unrelated individuals, were continuously employed full time but found it impossible to work their way out of poverty. Given that work for these households does not offer the promise of an adequate income, their continuing attachment to the labor force seems surprisingly strong.

The continuing efforts of millions of Americans to find jobs in slack labor markets also reflects a deep and lasting commitment to work. Even the manner in which we count the unemployed ensures that they are among the greatest devotees of work—by definition the unemployment statistics include only those who continue to search actively for employment, applying this test without regard for their specific job prospects. Those who decide the odds of finding work are too slim and give up on job search—the "discouraged workers"—are not counted as among the unemployed, even though they may have been forced into idleness. This willingness of the jobless to remain in the labor force in spite of prolonged unemployment testifies to the strength of work motivation on the fringes of the labor market.

*"I'm not listed as unemployed,
'cause I've stopped looking."*

It is curious that fears of a disintegrating work ethic continue to surface in an era of almost chronic labor surpluses. Over the past two decades, national unemployment rates have crept gradually upward, and the estimate of "full employment" in the American economy has risen from 4 percent unemployment under the Kennedy administration to at least 6 percent in the Reagan administration. These official targets do not count millions of Americans who are too discouraged to look for work or who are forced to accept part-time jobs, and yet the nation still has not approached full employment in any sense for nearly a decade. This persistent joblessness runs directly counter to claims of the imminent demise of work: it is difficult to argue that Americans are abandoning work in droves when the labor market is consistently unable to provide jobs for millions who desire work.

The surplus of labor in the national economy is not a new phenomenon—during most of the post-World War II period, the demand for labor has failed to keep pace with the supply of job seekers. No doubt, some portion of this unemployment is inevitable in a democratic society, as both employers and workers freely choose to accept or reject work situations. Yet the great bulk of unemployment is neither frictional nor voluntary. Due to whatever combination of structural barriers and governmental policies, the economy, though it has continued to expand, has failed to generate sufficient numbers of jobs in the aggregate or to produce a reasonable match between the skills of unemployed workers and emerging demands for labor.

In strict economic terms, unemployment today may not be the disaster it was in earlier periods. As part of a growing system of income supports, our affluent society has weakened the links between unemployment and poverty. These cushions—including old age and disability benefits, unemployment insurance, food stamps, medicaid, aid to families with dependent children and subsidized housing—provide assistance to the unemployed which enables them at least to keep body and soul together. Perhaps more importantly, the rise in female labor force participation and in the number of two-worker households softens the consequences of joblessness for many families—6 in 10 families have two or more wage earners. Just as employment does not guarantee an adequate income, unemployment is no longer synonymous with abject poverty.

Even when income losses are manageable, however, joblessness leaves the unemployed with few opportunities to satisfy the social and psychological needs which work typically fulfills. The welfare state may fulfill basic physical needs, but it does little for self-esteem and cannot provide the sense of dignity associated with gainful employment. These noneconomic motivations to work seem strong enough to prevent precipitous drops in work attachment even when workers are guaranteed incomes via transfer payments. In four major income support demonstration projects conducted in the United States, hours of work dropped by 1 to 8 percent among men while declining by roughly 20 percent among women. While these experiments were of limited duration and thus might not trigger more permanent changes in work habits, current research is consistent with the idea that work provides much more than a means of economic support.[7]

Expansion of Leisure and Nonwork Time

The only pervasive indications of a movement away from work is a slow but growing tendency for workers to forego further income gains in preference for greater amounts of paid leisure. Predictably, with greater affluence the higher marginal utility of leisure has caused many workers to trade wage and salary hikes for paid holidays and vacations. Taking more time away from the workplace to enjoy the fruits of their labor, Americans spend fewer hours per day, fewer days per year, and fewer years of their lives working than they did in the past. It is this trend, stemming not from any weakening commitment to work but from rational economic judgments of the relative value of income and leisure, which is reshaping the nature of work in the 1980s.

The shift toward greater leisure in itself is not a new phenomenon. In fact, the most spectacular shrinkage in worktime came in the early part of this century from declines in hours worked per week (Table 3-1). In 1900, the average nonagricultural worker put in 53 hours of work per week. By 1940, that number had fallen below 44. Since World War II, when the work ethic was supposed to have been on the decline, average hours worked per week in manufacturing with relatively few part-time workers have stabilized and the 40-hour workweek has become a surprisingly strong and universally recognized social norm. Clearly, while the recorded statistics of hours worked do not take into consideration the coffee breaks and other interruptions in work that are taken for granted in most American workplaces today, leisure gains are now secured in a manner different from the first half of this century.

Table 3-1

Decline in Average Weekly Hours of Work Has Slowed Since 1950

	Weekly Hours of Work						
	1981	1975	1970	1965	1960	1955	1950
Hours	38.1	38.7	39.6	40.5	40.5	41.6	41.7

	Weekly Hours of Work					
	1945	1940	1930	1920	1910	1900
Hours	46.1	43.9	47.7	49.8	52.1	53.2

Source: U.S. Bureau of Labor Statistics.

The recent decline in average hours worked can be traced partly to the growing numbers of workers who voluntarily spend only part of the customary workday or workweek on the job. From 1963 to 1981, such part-time workers grew in numbers from 8.8 million to 14.7 million, rising from 12 to nearly 14 percent of the workforce. This jump in part-time employment primarily reflects the influx of women into the labor force (they are three times as likely as men to seek part-time work), although increases in the numbers of young workers attending school and older workers seeking fewer hours have reinforced this trend (Figure 3.4). Full-time workers taken separately have gained only slightly more than one-half hour of weekly leisure in the past 13 years, averaging 42.4 hours of work per week in 1981.

This recent plateau in the workweek, however, has not halted the growth of leisure time for full-time workers. Since 1940, much of the gain in free time has come from decreases in the workyear achieved through both paid vacations and paid holidays. Before 1940, few nonmanagerial workers received paid vacations. By 1970, virtually all plant workers and office workers in metropolitan areas worked in establishments that provided paid vacations, with the average full-time worker receiving two full weeks. Similarly, the number of paid holidays has more than quadrupled in that time span, growing from an average of 2 days in 1940 to 9 days four decades later. Perhaps the most telling sign of workers' continuing appetite for leisure is that full-week vacations taken without pay rose between 1968 and 1979 from 14 to 20 percent of all vacations for men and from 34 to 39 percent for women.[8] It is this push for vacations and holidays plus the increase in part-time workers rather than shorter workweeks of full-time workers, which has reduced the average annual hours at work during the past four decades (Figure 3.4).

The rise in the number of families with two or more wage earners may add to the pressure for more time away from the

Figure 3.4   Average Annual Hours Spent at Work Has Declined By One-Third During the Century

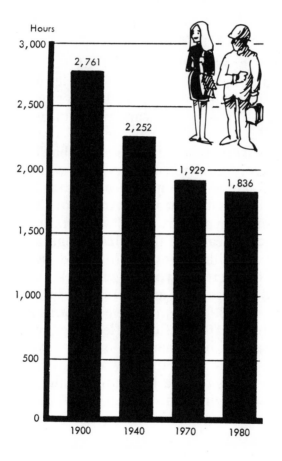

Source: Peter Henle, "Recent Growth of Paid Leisure for U.S. Workers," *Monthly Labor Review* (March 1962), pp. 249-257; Geoffrey H. Moore and Janice Neipert Hedges, "Trends in Labor and Leisure," *Monthly Labor Review* (February 1971), pp. 3-11; and *Economic Report to the President, 1981*, p. 274.

workplace. This push for greater leisure will be partially an outgrowth of the relative affluence of multiple income households, but it may also reflect an increasing pattern of husbands and wives sharing family responsibilities. This mutual acceptance of both provider and parenting roles would require an added measure of flexibility in work hours, and these emerging needs in the modern family may well be translated into future demands for paid leisure and shorter or more personalized work schedules.

There are few groups within the workforce who have not responded to the opportunity for greater leisure. Even the upward trend in total hours worked by women can be attributed entirely to new entrants and part-time workers in the labor force—the interest in paid leisure among full-time female workers as incomes rise parallels that of their male counterparts. Only dual job holders and overtime workers have continued to resist the appeal of greater leisure. Since 1956, when statistics on moonlighters were first compiled, between 4.5 and 5.5 percent of all workers have held two jobs, and in recent years the figure has remained around 5.0 percent with no evident downward trend. Similarly, the average hours of overtime worked per week in manufacturing has ranged between 2.4 and 3.9 in the last quarter century, hovering near 3.0.[9] Both these exceptions are easily explained—overtime effort often reflects employer steps to cope with variations in demand as much as worker desires for additional hours, and those workers who seek extra hours or second jobs tend to have low earnings and place a high value on marginal income gains. Balanced against evidence of shrinking workweeks and workyears, these limited cases only qualify slightly the broad trend toward more time free from the job.

In some sense, it is surprising that leisure has not made greater inroads into the world of work. During this century alone, productivity has at least quintupled—that increase means that a labor force of 20 million could produce the goods and services sufficient for the lifestyle that our ancestors enjoyed in "the golden nineties." Put in another way, if workers in 1982 were satisfied to live at the same standard of living as their parent did some three decades earlier, they could have cut the five-day workweek to three days or taken 20 weeks vacation per year. Needless to say, five-month vacations are not around the corner, but only because most workers choose steadily rising incomes over leisure gains. Since 1968, the share of potential pay raises translated into leisure growth has averaged roughly 16 percent for full-time employees.[10] This pattern of apportioning productivity gains between pecuniary benefits and leisure time ensures that, in terms of hours on the job, work is not soon to end.

The fear that Americans will abandon work has no rational basis, and can be advanced only when the many motivational forces which bring individuals to the workplace are ignored. People work for many different reasons, and even when growing affluence enables workers to obtain more leisure, such gains are taken in gradual increments of paid holidays and vacations. Labor force data suggest that Americans are working more, not less, opting for leisure only when that step is consistent with a continuing identification with established work roles. While the absolute economic need to work may diminish over time, the desire for relative income gains and the social and psychological functions of work persist. Those who anticipate a revolution against work are likely to be disappointed—even as both jobs and workers change, the great majority of Americans no doubt will continue to find reasons to work.

4 Tales of Work Dissatisfaction

> Without work all life goes
> rotten. But when work is
> soulless, life stifles and dies.
>
> —Albert Camus

Even though most Americans find reasons to remain in the labor force, their participation in itself reveals little about their satisfaction at the workplace. The persistence of reasonably tight labor markets and rising productivity lasting into the early 1970s focused new attention on this question of worker satisfaction in America. In many ways, this concern for the quality of work was a logical and appropriate outgrowth of increasing affluence. It seemed natural to expect that work provide not only a reliable and adequate income, but also a sense of satisfaction and personal fulfillment. When the realities of work in modern industrial society failed to match these rising expectations, the "problem" of worker alienation emerged.

In retrospect, it is hard to convey the intensity of the debate over work satisfaction or the fervor of warnings regarding worker discontent which surfaced in the early 1970s. Critics of the modern workplace not only perceived widespread dissatisfaction within the ranks of the employed, but they also feared a trend of rapid disintegration and decay. For example, some observers argued that "more and more workers—and every day this is more apparent—are becoming disenchanted with the boring, repetitive tasks set by a merciless assembly line or by bureaucracy."[1] More importantly, others feared that the prospect of spreading dissatisfaction threatened the very foundations of American democracy.[2] While few reacted with such total alarm, the issue eventually attracted national attention. The Secretary of Health, Education, and Welfare in the early 1970s ordered a review of the status of work in America, and President Richard Nixon proclaimed that "the most important part of the quality of life is the quality of work, and the new need for job satisfaction is the key to the quality of work."[3]

The themes of worker alienation and dissatisfaction had both intellectual and historical precedents—neither the ideas nor the psychological theories of human nature on which they were premised were particularly new. Yet fears of rampant discontent, based on reports of rising turnover, absenteeism, and disruption at the workplace, gained considerable credibility over the past decade. Most of the research supporting the presumed rise of work dissatisfaction offered scant evidence of any such trend, relying instead on anecdotes and narrow survey results to bolster visions of the alienated worker. However, the seriousness with which claims of sweeping discontent have been received suggests a need for a thorough review of the nature of satisfaction and discontent at the American workplace.

Sources of Alienation

The intellectual debate regarding dissatisfaction at the workplace has focused primarily on the concept of alienation. Although the use of the term "alienation" has varied considerably, the concept is commonly traced back to Karl Marx and to his discussions of the alienation of labor from capital and control over the means of production. Marx's view of alienation, unlike most contemporary versions, was deeply rooted in his critique of capitalism, focusing on issues of ownership and class structure rather than on the content and nature of work itself. Modern day proclaimers of worker discontent usually reject Marx's attack on the economic system, but they follow his descriptions of the impact of work on the alienated worker. Marx contended that man "does not fulfill himself in his work but denies himself, has a feeling of misery rather than well-being, does not develop freely his spiritual and physical powers but is physically exhausted and spiritually debased."[4] Certainly the image of the oppressive factory was vivid in Marx's mind in the mid-nineteenth century, and this perception continues to dominate discussions of dissatisfaction at the workplace today.

Contemporary stereotypes of the alienated worker reflect little of Marx's class consciousness, emphasizing the more subjective reactions of workers to the demands of their jobs. Thus, "alienation from work" is variously used to describe dissatisfaction with one's job, the experience of work as not intrinsically rewarding, and its experience as being insufficiently self-directed, meaningful, and self-expressive.[5] This view of alienation is intimately linked with the lack of opportunities for personal satisfaction:

> Alienation exists when workers are unable to control their immediate work processes, to develop a sense of purpose and function which connects their jobs to the overall organization of production, to belong to integrated industrial communities, and when they fail to become involved in the activity of work as a mode of personal self-expression.[6]

While Marx's definition of alienation emphasized the inherent relationship between labor and capital, more recent observers imply that a worker is "alienated" only when he *feels* detached, powerless, isolated or without purpose in his work. This subjective use of the term has rendered it virtually synonymous with generalized themes of work dissatisfaction and discontent.

Studies of work satisfaction since the 1930s have been grounded in this concept of alienation, but they have also been motivated by a more pragmatic belief that adjustments in working conditions or managerial structures might both enhance the contentment of workers and improve the productivity of industry. Few researchers have been concerned with abstract issues of work quality. Instead, most studies have sought to establish clear connections between work organization, worker attitudes and behavior, and overall labor productivity. The recent enthusiasm for discussions of work quality and worker participation stems from this belief that both workers and employers will gain—the hope being that increases in work satisfaction and labor productivity will be intimately linked. The potential for cooperation between labor and management is stressed throughout the literature as an argument for work reform even in the absence of evidence that work dissatisfaction is a serious problem.

The concept of alienation has been employed in one other sense, as a description of the impact of modern technological change on the quality of work. For example, Jacques Ellul described today's work as molded by technological advance, rendering it by nature "an aimless, useless, and callous business, tied to a clock, an absurdity profoundly felt and resented by the workers."[7] In the same vein, a popular writer viewed problems of meaningless work and alienation as inherent in traditional industrial societies and perhaps wholly unresolvable given current production technologies.[8] Even those who do not subscribe to theories of technological determinism often acknowledge the "general alienating tendencies" of modern industrial organizations and technologies.[9] However, this latter group is distinguished by their belief that "alienating work" can be eliminated, vigorously contending that the quality of work can be improved through reform efforts in spite of the effects of technological change.

Expectations and Human Nature

In examining claims of worker discontent, it is important to consider more than the nature of work itself. No job—regardless of its content—is *inherently* boring or challenging. Work satisfaction is necessarily a subjective reaction to the job, reflecting the degree of harmony between job demands, personal expectations and individual needs. Some may indeed seek exciting responsibilities at the workplace, but others may expect or desire little from the job. This highly personalized aspect of work satisfaction is seldom addressed by work reform advocates who rely heavily on speculations regarding human nature to support claims of dissatisfaction at the workplace.

The view of human nature which has come to dominate the debate on work satisfaction and work reform was formulated by psychologist Abraham Maslow. In 1954, Maslow set forth in *Motivation and Personality* a theory of human motivation and behavior based on a hierarchy of human needs. At the lowest and most immediate level, Maslow claimed that physical or survival needs are operative. If these needs are satisfied, higher order needs presumably come into play—for example, recognition and acceptance by peers and other social needs. Finally, if these needs are also fulfilled, the individual seeks the ultimate goals of self-realization and spiritual development. Maslow argued that, while individuals may reach various levels in the hierarchy, they all follow a similar progression of needs in their personal development.

At any level of the hierarchy of needs, the failure to satisfy the operative need will supposedly generate frustration and discontent. More importantly, the satisfaction of each lower level need generates wants of the next highest order. Although low-level needs must always be satisfied first, their complete fulfillment cannot sustain individual satisfaction, leading inevitably to new desires. In Maslow's framework, enduring satisfaction can only be achieved through the fulfillment of higher order needs.

HIGHER ORDER NEEDS

Maslow's scale of needs has obvious relevance to those interested in finding new ways to motivate workers, and his ideas have gained wide acceptance among industrial psychologists. Numerous experiments and studies were conducted in the 1950s and 1960s in an attempt to refine Maslow's hypotheses, and to develop specific correlations between work attributes and worker satisfaction which could be used as a guide for work reform efforts. Maslow's work has provided the theoretical basis for the shift away from an exclusive emphasis on economic and other extrinsic rewards of work as a means of increasing satisfaction and work effort within the labor force.

Most contemporary theories of management and work satisfaction are based to some extent on Maslow's hierarchy of needs. The ideas of Frederick Herzberg and Douglas McGregor have enjoyed the widest acceptance and application in the United States. Both Herzberg and McGregor focused on the implications of Maslow's view of human needs for effective labor-management relations, arguing that traditional attempts to motivate workers failed to meet and capitalize upon their higher order needs. Their original research dealt with white-collar workers, but subsequent studies attempted to extend their theories to many other work settings. In spite of limitations encountered in developing models of motivation and behavior applicable to all workers, Herzberg and McGregor have played an important role in broadening the scope of the debate over worker needs and sources of satisfaction.

Herzberg's theory of work satisfaction was based on research findings indicating that the variables linked to worker *discontent* were separate and distinct from those tied to work *satisfaction.*[10] He suggested that traditional rewards for work—money, good working conditions, and leisure time—could not truly motivate workers. True motivators, Herzberg claimed, are those job attributes which stimulate individual growth and fulfill Maslow's higher order needs for recognition, achievement, and responsibility. Traditional rewards, which Herzberg termed hygiene factors, could produce apathetic workers at best, while only enriched or autonomous work roles could sustain motivated workers.

Douglas McGregor approached the problems of work motivation and satisfaction from a slightly different perspective, but reached similar conclusions regarding the importance of appeals to higher order needs. McGregor examined two alternative theories of personnel management, which he labeled theory X and theory Y.[11] Theory X, the traditional management style, held that workers prefer limited responsibility and greater security, inherently dislike work and can be motivated only by coercion, control, and punishment. Theory Y portrayed workers as naturally desiring work and responsibility, and as being best motivated by challenging work which used their capabilities fully. McGregor believed that most jobs did not fully challenge workers, and that theory X management styles failed to capitalize on their natural inclinations to work. Redesigned organizations and broader, more autonomous jobs along the lines of theory Y presumably could evoke greater work efforts.

The relatively optimistic views of human nature underlying the work of Maslow, Herzberg and McGregor—the image of workers as reaching for ever-higher goals—have led many to prejudge reactions to work. For example, a public opinion analyst has concluded that when jobs do not offer opportunities for self-fulfillment, workers "retaliate by holding back their commitment, if not their labor."[12] French social philosopher Ellul opined ". . . it is in work that human beings develop and affirm their personality. . . . When the human being is no longer responsible for his work and no longer figures in it, he feels spiritually outraged."[13] In these and many other instances, Maslow's observation that many individuals never reach the pursuit of higher order needs seems forgotten.

Nevertheless, attacks on the modern workplace have flourished. Although the evidence may not be persuasive, some critics have found presumed signs of worker withdrawal, resentment and dissatisfaction, warning of potential declines in productivity growth as a result.[14] Others have cited alleged declines in work discipline, motivation and satisfaction, claiming that workers suffer "a loss of individuality, dignity and self-respect."[15] The range of problems associated with perceived drops in work satisfaction is overwhelming: increases in job turnover, absenteeism, strikes and work-related accidents; deterioration of product quality, production standards, worker mental health and discipline; heightened feelings of isolation and political impotence among workers; and declines in national economic growth and the quality of life. Yet little serious research has been undertaken to document these trends or to establish causal relationships between perceived problems and issues of work satisfaction. In the absence of such evidence, tales of work dissatisfaction provide topics of interesting speculation but an inadequate basis for making work reform a high priority in labor policy.

Examining Trends at Work

The search for "hard" data to support claims of widespread or growing dissatisfaction cannot avoid assumptions about the causal relationships between worker attitudes and behavior. In the literature on worker dissatisfaction, higher quit rates, absenteeism, accident-frequency rates, and increased disruptions through strikes and other work stoppages are all assumed to be expressions of worker discontent. These causal connections are extremely difficult to prove, but strong trends in such areas at least would lend greater plausibility to assertions of rising dissatisfaction at the workplace. If job turnover were on the upswing, for instance, one would have to account for such changes in other ways before dismissing themes of worker discontent.

Unfortunately for critics of the modern workplace, the measurable evidence in support of theories of worker alienation is surprisingly weak and mostly anecdotal. Even without questioning the presumed causal relationships between work satisfaction and behavior, employment data generally provide little basis for contentions of shifting work patterns stemming from worker discontent. Where changes in labor market trends are significant, more obvious and immediate explanations abound. Otherwise, the data demonstrate far more continuity than change.

Data on job turnover in studies of work satisfaction provide a useful example. The frequency with which workers quit their jobs may seem related to satisfaction at work, but historical trends suggest that overall employment conditions are far more important as a factor in fluctuating turnover rates. Regardless of their relative satisfaction or discontent, workers are more likely to leave their jobs in tight labor markets, while holding on to their positions during periods of high unemployment (Figure 4.1). George Strauss undertook an exhaustive review of fluctuations in quit rates between 1958 and 1972, and concluded that "practically all of the variations can be explained by changes in factors such as unemployment, relative hours and earnings rates, and the age, sex, and racial composition of the workforce."[16] When econometric analysis is used to control for these factors, the remaining variations in turnover rates which could be attributed to work dissatisfaction are not significant.

Labor market trends in other areas also offer meager support for claims of burgeoning discontent among American workers. Rates of absenteeism for U.S. workers have shown no significant trend in recent years, declining slightly during the 1974-75 recession but generally remaining stable throughout the decade at 3.5 percent of usual full-time hours.[17] Incidence rates for occupational injury and illness have climbed slightly since 1973, but are likely to reflect federal regulations generating better statistics rather than more industrial accidents. Wage-related concerns continue to dominate union-management disputes—accounting annually since 1969 for 55 to 85 percent of all time lost in strikes—and the percent of total working time lost due to work stoppages in the late 1970s was among the lowest levels of the postwar period, with no discernible upward trend.[18] Strikes associated with issues most directly related to job content (division of work, supervision, workload, work rules and assignments) have rarely caused more than 5 percent of

Figure 4.1 Manufacturing Quit Rates Rise When Unemployment Falls

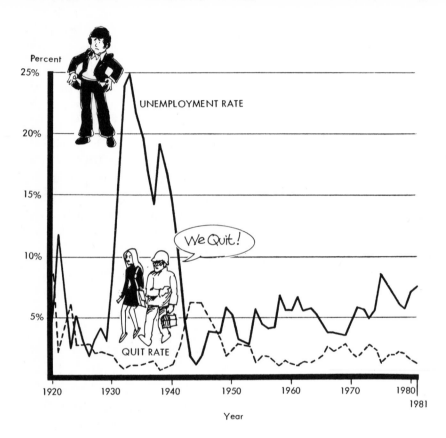

Source: U.S. Bureau of the Census, *Historical Statistics of the United States, Colonial Times to 1970* (Washington: U.S. Government Printing Office, 1975), pp. 181-182; and U.S. Bureau of Labor Statistics, *Employment and Earnings,* January 1982, pp. 133, 138.

total days idle in any given year, and also have not perceptibly increased.

Recognizing that current labor market trends, with their tenuous causal connection to worker alienation, offer minimal support, critics of the workplace more frequently rely on survey results and other subjective measures of dissatisfaction to bolster claims of rising worker discontent. The attempt to gauge worker feelings and reactions is certainly legitimate, but it also raises a morass of questions regarding the objectivity of survey methodologies and the significance of poll results. Only a careful review of survey approaches can reconcile conflicting results and provide a persuasive assessment of the relative satisfaction of American workers.

Are Workers Miserably Content?

At first glance, the scores of surveys on work satisfaction appear rife with contradictions. Taken in the aggregate, they seem to portray workers as both satisfied with their jobs and unhappy in their work. The survey results and conclusions depend to a great extent on the methodology employed—how questions are phrased and what feelings or attitudes are viewed as relevant to an individual's satisfaction with work. If one fails to look beyond superficial reports, survey results appear wholly contradictory and confusion reigns.

One approach to measuring worker discontent is simply to ask people how satisfied they are with their jobs. This basic methodology has been employed for over three decades, and the findings of Gallup polls and other surveys of this type provide the only longitudinal data available on work satisfaction. The results of these surveys have been amazingly constant over time: between 81 and 92 percent of all workers have consistently reported that they are generally satisfied with the work they do (Table 4-1). The remaining portion of the labor force expressing dissatisfaction should not be forgotten, but this relatively high level of reported contentment clashes sharply with the assumptions of those who have viewed work trends with increasing alarm.

Table 4-1   Most Workers Are Generally "Satisfied" With Their Work

Year	Source[1]	Percent satisfied
1958	Survey Research Center[2]	81
1962	National Opinion Research Center	83
1963	Gallup Poll[2]	89
1964	Survey Research Center (University of California)	91
1964	National Opinion Research Center[2]	92
1965	Gallup Poll[2]	87
1966	Gallup Poll[2]	92
1966	Gallup Poll[2]	89
1969	Survey Research Center	85
1969	Gallup Poll[2]	92
1971	Survey Research Center	91
1971	Gallup Poll[2]	88
1971	Gallup Poll[2]	86
1973	Gallup Poll[2]	88
1973	Survey Research Center	90
1974	National Opinion Research Center	85
1975	National Opinion Research Center	87
1976	National Opinion Research Center	86
1977	Survey Research Center	88
1978	National Opinion Research Center	87
1980	National Opinion Research Center	83
1981	Los Angeles Times	92

1. Wording of questions and nature of sample vary by source, possibly affecting results.

2. Sample includes males only; all others include both sexes.

A more complex series of work satisfaction studies has focused on correlations between overall job satisfaction and various aspects of an individual's employment. In this framework, researchers have been concerned less with the level of overall satisfaction expressed by workers than with the specific job attributes which seem to enhance satisfaction. These studies are of particular importance to advocates of "challenging" work, for they directly address the question of what matters to workers.

The survey results do not render a clear verdict on the origins of work satisfaction. Numerous job attributes—both related and irrelevant to the intrinsic nature of work—have been shown to be of some significance to the overall satisfaction of workers. Perhaps the most exhaustive attempt to link job attributes and work satisfaction, conducted by the University of Michigan's Survey Research Center in 1969, suggested that aspects of supervision and the work environment are at least as important as the nature of the job itself in fostering work satisfaction (Table 4-2). Subsequent analyses conducted in 1973 and 1977 confirmed the conclusion that adequate resources (including supervision) to do a job well were as closely linked to work satisfaction as the level of challenge intrinsic in any particular type of work.[19]

When survey methodologies are changed, however, the apparent relationships between attributes and overall job satisfaction also shift. The University of Michigan Survey Research Center correlated measures of overall job satisfaction with worker statements regarding the most positive aspects of their jobs. In contrast, the 1971 study by Sheppard and Herrick asked respondents if their jobs included a number of presumably desirable qualities (e.g., opportunities for growth, interesting work), and if they were bothered by the absence of any such qualities. The methodology of the latter study contained a much greater emphasis on intrinsic work rewards than the earlier Michigan study, and solicited negative rather than positive statements about work from its respondents. Predictably, Sheppard and Herrick's findings indicated a stronger role for the content of jobs in determining work satisfaction.

Table 4-2 Good Supervision Is At Least As Important As the Nature of Work Itself

	Correlation with overall job satisfaction
Supervision	
Having a supervisor who takes a personal interest in those he/she supervises and goes out of his/her way to praise good work (N = 1237)	.37
Receiving adequate help, assistance, authority, time, information, machinery, tools and equipment to do the job (N = 1494)	.32
Having a supervisor who does not supervise too closely (N = 1246)	.30
Job content	
Having autonomy in deciding matters that affect one's work (N = 1508)	.28
Having a job with "enriching" demands (e.g., a job that demands that one learn new things, have a high level of skill, be creative, and do a variety of different things) (N = 1509)	.26

Source: University of Michigan, Survey Research Center, *Survey of Working Conditions, November 1970* (Washington: U.S. Government Printing Office, 1971), p. 432.

It is not that there are "right" and "wrong" ways to gauge satisfaction in worker surveys. One simply must wonder whether research findings of this nature mirror the structure of surveys more than they reflect the attitudes of workers. The great majority of workers indicate they are satisfied with their work, but when asked if they would choose the same jobs again, the percentage of positive responses drops sharply.[20] Similarly, while good pay continues to correlate highly with job satisfaction, over three-fourths of all Americans say they would refuse to leave an enjoyable job for one that pays more.[21] Does this mean that workers are content, miserable, or merely resigned to their current roles? It depends to a great extent on how and what they are asked.

Some correlations between job satisfaction and demographic characteristics seem relatively clear—satisfaction generally increases with age and income, tends to be higher among whites than among blacks, and is less common among blue-collar workers above age 30 than among white-collar employees in similar age groups. As George Strauss notes, "there is [also] considerable evidence that, at least for some workers, dissatisfaction is directly related to short job cycles, surface-attention work, low autonomy and control of the pace of work, and the lack of challenge."[22] Beyond these basic principles, there is broad room for interpretation; yet any coherent and defensible view of work satisfaction must attempt to account for variations in survey results, and must be firmly rooted in realistic images of the nature of workers and their jobs in contemporary society.

A Look at Methodology

By necessity, work satisfaction surveys assume that the subjective responses of workers accurately reflect their thoughts and feelings regarding work. While there are few alternatives in exploring job satisfaction, this self-reporting of attitudes is plagued by methodological shortcomings. In particular, there is reason to believe that surveys on work satisfaction may (1) reflect attempts to maintain self-esteem rather than the actual feelings of workers; (2) fail to measure the full diversity of worker needs and expectations in gauging job satisfaction; and (3) assume causal relationships between work and personal satisfaction which are subject to question. These three general concerns provide a basis for understanding the apparent contradictions in recent research findings on satisfaction at the workplace.

The importance of work to self-esteem poses the greatest problem for survey methodologies. The instinct to protect a positive self-image can lead in many directions, depending on the structure and phraseology of survey questions. Workers may wish to seem generally satisfied at work, lest they offer appearances of failure or resignation; however, when asked about specific work attributes, a concern for self-esteem could bolster incentives to "blame" the job for not utilizing their full potential. Thus, many workers can be both content with their jobs and "bothered" by the lack of autonomy, responsibility or challenge at work. There is no real contradiction—the knowledge that jobs are *supposed* to be satisfying, interesting, and challenging simply encourages us to react differently to questions of overall satisfaction than to inquiries regarding the adequacy of specific job attributes.

The limitations of subjective indices of work satisfaction have been acknowledged by most analysts, although usually in attempts to disarm their critics. A cogent treatment of the problems inherent in self-reporting is found in George Strauss' critique of research on work satisfaction:

> There is no reason to believe that attitude questions are answered with complete honesty or that conscious—or even unconscious—attitudes accurately reflect a worker's objective situation. When a

worker reports that he is 'satisfied' with his job, it may mean only that his self-respect forces him to answer this way; . . . This is not an attempt to deceive the interviewer; one's need for mental balance (to reduce cognitive dissonance) may require one to believe that he is really satisfied.[23]

Depending on the question posed, the link between work and self-esteem can create an exaggerated sense of satisfaction at the workplace, or an underestimation of worker contentment with uninteresting or unchallenging tasks. The observation that feelings are "escape routes," ways of coping with and manipulating one's environment, has profound implications for the study of work satisfaction.[24]

In a similar manner, the usefulness of surveys in gauging work satisfaction is limited by the inability to incorporate the diversity of personal expectations and needs into a useful research methodology. The discovery that many jobs are repetitive, unchallenging, or devoid of opportunities for personal growth in itself tells us nothing about the satisfaction of workers—they may expect nothing more from their jobs, or actually appreciate the absence of strenuous demands. There are many substitutes for an appreciation of the intrinsic nature of one's work, ranging from social life in a community of workers to economic security and the pursuit of leisure. The fundamental determinant of work satisfaction is the degree of harmony between job attributes and worker expectations, with both perceptions of the nature of work and the hopes or needs of workers varying tremendously. Analyses which portray the workforce as filled with aspiring psychologists and sociologists project a set of values which ignores the true richness and diversity of human aspirations.

The temptation to view all workers as seeking fulfillment or self-actualization stems from a misinterpretation of the work of Maslow, and perhaps even from flaws within the original theory itself. Contrary to the concept of a self-propelling hierarchy of needs, David McClelland and others suggest that people differ considerably in their needs and priorities. They do not necessarily pursue "higher order" needs when more immediate ones are reasonably satisfied, and studies reveal that many workers prefer working with their hands rather than their heads.[25] Yet the methodology implicit in work satisfaction survey data does not respond effectively to this diversity of workers. Even when research designs have attempted to assess worker expectations and disappointments, the survey questions are biased—again, to ask if one is bothered by the limitations of a job or hoped for more is to touch upon one's self-image and provoke a defensive response.

Finally, assumptions of causality also render the methodology of work satisfaction research vulnerable to criticism. Virtually all surveys assume that work attributes serve as a causal factor in determining levels of satisfaction in varying job roles, but it is equally plausible that an individual's level of satisfaction influences the choice of jobs or work roles.[26] Thus, the traditional assumption of causality which posits work satisfaction as the dependent variable is not self-evident; more importantly, a reversal of this assumption would invalidate most work satisfaction studies. While polling techniques can contribute to our knowledge of worker attitudes, these criticisms of survey methodologies suggest the need for considerable caution in the use and interpretation of findings regarding work satisfaction.

A Realistic View of Work Satisfaction

The research of critics of the modern workplace has played an important role in updating the historical context for understanding worker needs, albeit at the risk of overstating the importance of job content and attributes. In an affluent society with large discretionary incomes and rising expectations, adequate pay and working conditions are no longer the sole factors influencing work satisfaction. A balanced and realistic view of work satisfaction, one consistent with the bulk of current research findings, must recognize that there is no single determinant of relative contentment at work. As we might guess, the evidence suggests that most Americans now bring a wide array of needs and expectations to the workplace, and their "satisfaction" is a composite of reactions and feelings to the many aspects of their job. Indeed, similar conditions have prevailed from time immemorial. Jacob's working conditions, the Bible tells us, were harsh and the wages were meager, but the nonpecuniary rewards of his labor were adequate to keep him on the job for 14 years.

This is not to say that the adequacy of salaries and wages has lost its importance in the labor market. To the contrary, there are strong indications that most workers continue to place a major emphasis on traditional work rewards, at least until reaching a level of considerable affluence. The data from the University of Michigan Survey Research Center showed that in every age, occupation, marital, or educational category, those with incomes under $5,000 (in 1969) were more than twice as likely to be dissatisfied as those with incomes above $10,000. Both the likelihood that men will work second jobs and that women will enter the labor force decrease as incomes rise, and workers' decisions to retire are based heavily on the adequacy of pension or other retirement benefits. Even industry quit rates reflect the significance of income as a factor in job satisfaction: in 1981, the three durable goods manufacturing industries with the lowest wages had the highest quit rates, preserving a strong inverse relationship between wage levels and quit rates which has held true in both durable and nondurable goods manufacturing for many years.

Perhaps the most significant expressions of priorities from workers themselves suggest that pay has retained a dominant position among job attributes. While labor unions may underemphasize issues of work quality, wages nonetheless continue to be the central issue in most labor disputes—in recent years, almost two of three days lost in strikes were the result of battles over wages and benefits. In the same vein, a 1977 opinion survey revealed that more than three-fourths of workers who responded would prefer a 10 percent raise over more interesting work.[27] Clearly, many workers have not reached an income level where they would be willing to trade higher wages for greater intrinsic rewards at work, causing union leaders to conclude, "If you want to enrich the job, enrich the paycheck."[28]

The awareness that wages are important neither denies that many jobs are unrewarding nor asserts that workers holding unpleasant jobs are happy. It simply serves to question the assumption that workers would sacrifice much of their pay for "better quality" work. This attachment of workers to what they perceive as a better standard of living must give pause to those who would "improve" work quality by shifting resources to work reform experiments.

In light of the truly "dehumanizing" nature of some jobs, particularly in machine-dominated industries, it is surprising that workers are able to derive any satisfaction from their work. Yet sociological studies of the most trying work settings have shown that people can find pleasure at work, even when they fail to derive satisfaction from the content of their jobs. Workers frequently respond to the miseries of tedious or distasteful tasks by creating an informal community at the workplace, fulfilling social needs which may be at least as important as occupational goals. Goran Palm vividly portrays the phenomenon:

> It is precisely when work is felt to be joyless and inhuman that the need for joy and human contact becomes so palpable that it breaks out where one least expects it. In the midst of drudgery. As a powerful counteracting force; as a means of protest and enduring; as unexpected dandelions on an asphalted road.[29]

No doubt the search for community is a means of adapting, of adjusting and surviving. While not an argument for unrewarding work, this solidarity among workers does help explain why Americans are not abandoning factories in droves. Rather than emphasizing the nature of their jobs, workers will make family and friends the focus of their lives.

The capacity to adapt to repetitive or uninteresting work has been viewed by critics of the workplace with mixed emotions. Calling this capacity "remarkable," one perceptive analyst goes on to argue that the demands of work are probably fairly consonant with the values and aspirations of the blue-collar labor force, and that the typical worker with an "alienating" job is probably satisfied with a life organized around leisure, family and consumption.[30] Others take a far more pessimistic view of the capacity for adaptation, one which emphasizes necessity and oppression:

> . . . the constant exercise of impersonal labor has resulted in the total depersonalization of the laborer. He has been shaped by his work, used by it, mechanized, and assimilated.[31]

In this sense, the ability and willingness of workers to adapt to unrewarding work is both their salvation and their curse—helping them to survive work which they have no choice but to accept, while also ensuring the continued presence of such work in the labor market by virtue of their willingness to accept it. With both the needs and the choices of many workers thus limited, harsh work is not soon to disappear.

The aggregate level of dissatisfaction in the labor force stemming from unrewarding work remains difficult to measure with any certainty. There are some horrible jobs to be filled, and no doubt there are many workers who are generally unhappy with their lot. Yet the case for viewing the American workforce as a teeming mass of discontent is unconvincing. The great majority of American workers probably fall somewhere in the middle, feeling generally "satisfied" with their jobs and yet always finding aspects of work they would love to change. More importantly, these middle ranks are not likely to dwindle substantially—the great diversity of needs and hopes brought to the workplace virtually guarantees reactions of partial fulfillment, and basic human ambivalence toward work ensures some degree of mixed feelings. Just as our imperfect labor market fails to provide work for all members of the labor force, it also falls short of a perfect match between worker expectations and job demands. And so the love-hate relationship with work continues.

Even if we reject images of a workforce burgeoning with discontent, the quality of work in America may still be a source of legitimate concern. If there were clear indications that work was becoming harsher or less challenging over time, that certainly would be cause for alarm. Furthermore, if the potential for redesigning jobs and reforming the workplace seemed great, humanitarian concerns alone would compel us to act. The critics of the modern workplace have made an important contribution to labor policy by raising these implicit questions. The future of their cause will depend largely on whether we believe the problem is growing more serious, and whether we believe we can significantly change the outcome at costs society would be willing to pay.

5 The Changing Nature of Work

> After you've done a thing the
> same way for two years, look
> it over carefully. After five
> years, look at it with suspicion.
> And after ten years, throw it
> away and start all over.
>
> —Alfred Edward Perlman,
> former president of New
> York Central Railroad

One way of examining whether the "problem" of work satisfaction is growing more serious is by assessing the ever-changing nature of work itself. Today's jobs are considerably different from those of a century ago and even a few decades ago, with some work roles dwindling as new ones emerge. We have fewer farmers but more computer specialists than ever before. Even if the "habit" of working hasn't changed much, the experience of working and the demands of the labor market may have little in common with that of prior generations.

The nature of work constitutes only half of the work satisfaction equation, with the hopes and expectations of workers carrying at least equal importance. Yet trends in the content and structure of work—including changes in the work environment, in skill requirements, and in the degree of worker autonomy and control—do set limits for potential satisfaction at the workplace. If growing segments of the labor force are pushed into jobs characterized by repetitive or unrewarding tasks, the threat of growing discontent among workers must be taken seriously. In contrast, if skill requirements in the labor market are rising and employment in harsh or unpleasant occupations falling, claims of burgeoning dissatisfaction in the modern workforce become much less plausible.

The most visible trends in the nature of work, such as the overall shift toward white-collar and service employment, tell us surprisingly little about prospects for work satisfaction among future generations of workers. Yet if we look beyond these generalizations, there are some encouraging signs—the percentage of unskilled jobs has declined steadily, the most boring and punishing tasks have disappeared and those that survive are increasingly being done by machines rather than men. There also remain some disconcerting trends, including the lack of uniform gains in skill requirements and the threat of displacement of low-skilled workers through automation and rapid technological innovation. These changes do not eliminate possibilities for satisfaction at the workplace, but they do threaten to disrupt the lives of many workers during a period of painful readjustment.

The Growth of the Service Sector

Classic critiques of industrial work are increasingly misdirected, for they focus more on anachronisms than on current labor market conditions. By weight of numbers, secretaries now deserve more scrutiny than autoworkers. Public schoolteachers outnumber all the production workers in the chemical, oil, rubber, plastic, paper and steel industries combined. Just as the industrial revolution reduced the portion of American workers laboring on farms from over 40 percent to less than 3 percent, a contemporary transformation of work is steadily undermining the relative importance of manufacturing as a generator of jobs. The office is replacing the factory as the most common workplace, and employment is shifting to the service sector of the economy with ever-increasing speed (Figure 5.1).

These broad occupational trends are not newly discovered—in fact, references to the burgeoning service sector have become so frequent as to seem trite. Agriculture, manufacturing and mining, which once dictated the basic structure of the labor market, no longer represent the typical workplace. A sizable and growing segment of the population does not have even a secondary relationship to the production or distribution of goods, instead providing an array of services of unprecedented scope and diversity. In the United States, growth in the service sector accounted for 84 percent of all additional jobs created in the three decades following 1950, and virtually every major industrial country in the world now has at least half its labor force in this tertiary sector.[1] These trends emphasize that, while the problems of the assembly line remain a source of concern, the nature of work in service industries will have a greater role in shaping future trends in job satisfaction.

Figure 5.1 Employment Has Shifted Steadily Toward the Service Sector

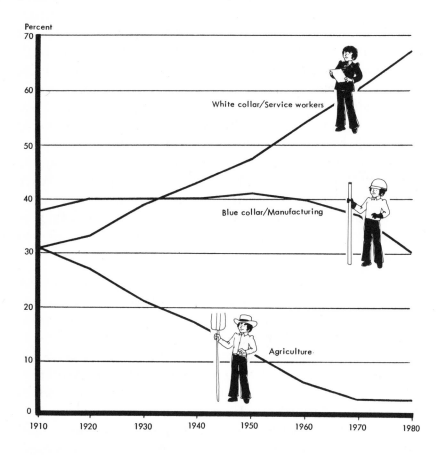

Percent

White collar/Service workers

Blue collar/Manufacturing

Agriculture

Source: U.S. Bureau of the Census, *Historical Statistics of the United States, Colonial Times to 1970* (Washington: U.S. Government Printing Office, 1975), p. 139; and U.S. Bureau of Labor Statistics, *Employment and Earnings,* January 1981, pp. 180-181.

The shift toward service employment is in many ways a direct result of rising affluence and technological advance. With machine-supported manufacturing requiring a declining share of the nation's overall work effort, Americans have been able to purchase and to provide services which earlier generations never contemplated. No doubt, the surge of women into the labor force has strengthened this demand for personal services, but increasing affluence alone would have aroused a growing appetite for the many amenities of a service economy. Aided by technological advances in fields ranging from health care to home entertainment, the growth of the service sector is now altering our most basic concepts of work and destroying traditional links between work and physical effort. Increasingly, we engage in "abstract" work with symbols instead of tools, producing reports rather than making bread. Only an affluent society could afford the luxury of freeing so many of its workers from the production process.

Along with the shift from the manufacturing to the service sector, a parallel transformation of the labor market can be seen in the movement from blue-collar to white-collar employment (Table 5-1). Farming was the most common occupation in 1900 and blue-collar workers were most numerous in 1940, but by 1981 slightly more than half of the workforce held white-collar jobs. In 1900, unskilled laborers outnumbered managers and professionals, household servants were more common than professionals, and unskilled workers filled one-third of all blue-collar jobs. In contrast, managers and professionals today outnumber unskilled laborers five to one, professionals are 10 times more prevalent than household servants, and craftsmen and semiskilled workers comprise nearly 90 percent of the blue-collar workforce. The long term trend is clear—white-collar employment has grown dramatically at the expense of farm and unskilled blue-collar work.

Table 5-1 Occupational Distribution from 1900 to 1981

Occupation	1981	1960	1940	1920	1900
White collar:	52.7%	43.3%	31.1%	24.9%	17.6%
Professional and technical	16.3	11.8	7.5	5.4	4.3
Managers and administrators	11.5	8.8	7.3	6.6	5.8
Clerical	18.5	15.1	9.6	8.0	3.0
Sales	6.4	7.6	6.7	4.9	4.5
Blue collar:	31.1	38.6	39.8	40.2	35.8
Craft	12.6	14.2	12.0	13.0	10.5
Operatives	14.0	19.4	18.4	15.6	12.8
Nonfarm laborers	4.5	5.0	9.4	11.6	12.5
Services	13.4	11.6	11.7	7.8	9.0
Private households	1.0	2.8	4.7	3.3	5.4
Farm workers	2.8	6.4	17.4	27.0	37.5

Source: David L. Kaplan and M. Claire Casey, *Occupational Trends in the United States, 1900 to 1950* (Washington: U.S. Government Printing Office, 1958); U.S. Bureau of the Census, *United States Census of the Population, 1960, Occupational Characteristics* (Washington: U.S. Government Printing Office, 1963); U.S. Bureau of the Census, *1970 Census of the Population, Occupation by Industry* (Washington: U.S. Government Printing Office, 1972); and *Employment and Earnings,* January 1982, p. 164.

Part of this growth in professional and managerial ranks reflects the increasing size and complexity of organizations, as well as the growing importance of research and managerial functions in the use of advanced technologies. Yet some portion of this surge in white-collar employment must also be viewed as "non-essential"—a host of vice presidents, special assistants and consultants once considered unnecessary now thrive in an affluent society. For example, the ratio of nonproduction to production workers in manufacturing has doubled in less than four decades, from 14 percent in 1943 to 28 percent in 1978, demonstrating that the requirement to mobilize for maximum production during World War II rendered substantial managerial layers expendable. Staffing patterns in the military reflect a similar trend: with armed forces of 2.1 million, we now have more admirals and generals than during the last world war when our forces totalled 12 million. Of course, judgments regarding "necessary" staffing levels are always relative, and the growth of professional and managerial ranks may generate qualitative improvements not easily measured through statistical data. Even in this context, however, the economy appears "featherbedded" with jobs which could not be supported by a less wealthy society.

Better Or Just Cleaner?

Intuitively, these trends toward white-collar jobs and service employment seem to reflect improvements in the quality of work. Yet such quick reactions to the potential for job satisfaction stem more from our biases regarding social class and status than from any realistic assessment of changes in the nature of work. In particular, the terms "white-collar" and "blue-collar" offer no relative assessment of requisite job skills, and are a reflection of

> . . . a system of social stratification that regards office work as a higher-status occupation than factory work, administration as more prestigious than manual labor, or, indeed, any occupation related directly to the production of goods.[2]

A closer look at our "white-collar" and "blue-collar" categories reveals a wide range of skill levels, work environments and job attributes in both groups, telling us very little about the likelihood of job satisfaction in white-collar versus blue-collar roles.

Ultimately, the simplistic dichotomy of "white-collar" and "blue-collar" employment masks as much as it reveals. Neither term provides a meaningful basis for categorizing the nature of various jobs—often the distinction reflects little more than the relative cleanliness of work settings. Many blue-collar jobs actually require more skill and provide more challenge than white-collar roles, and the shift toward white-collar employment may represent more of a lateral movement than an improvement in work quality. While clerical workers may enjoy a more pleasant environment, the tasks of a skilled craftsman in the factory demand more talent and engender more pride. By their nature, classifications which lump together mailmen and physicists, tool and diemakers and sweepers, are not useful predictors of work content or of the potential for satisfaction on the job.

The shift toward the service sector offers even fewer clues regarding prospects for work satisfaction, again because of the broad range of jobs encompassed by the category. While many police detectives and *haute cuisine* chefs may be challenged by their work, the bulk of service jobs are not of such high quality. The legions of janitors, dishwashers and hospital attendants at the bottom of the wage scale normally perform the most unpleasant and tedious tasks, and the advantages of their lot compared to that of factory workers are hard to see. Certainly many service workers enjoy less status and lower pay than their counterparts on the assembly line, fulfilling roles associated with servility and held in low esteem. While more adequate wages for those in the worst service jobs would alleviate some of these concerns, employment in the service sector surely is no guarantee of a fate better than that suffered in segments of blue-collar manufacturing.

If increases in white-collar and service employment are poor indicators of prospects for job satisfaction, part of the reason may be that structural changes in the labor market point in many directions. A comparison of recent occupational shifts with past trends in job satisfaction by occupation provides a useful illustration (Figure 5.2). Within expanding occupational sectors, professionals and managers

Figure 5.2 Employment Growth Is Occurring in Occupations with Both High and Low Historical Levels of Job Satisfaction

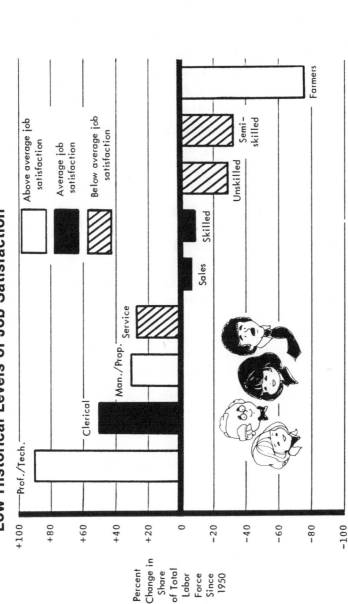

Above average job satisfaction

Average job satisfaction

Below average job satisfaction

Prof./Tech.

Clerical

Man./Prop.

Service

Sales

Skilled

Unskilled

Semi-skilled

Farmers

Percent Change in Share of Total Labor Force Since 1950

+100
+80
+60
+40
+20
0
−20
−40
−60
−80
−100

Source: Average job satisfaction by occupation derived from Robert P. Quinn and Graham L. Staines, *The 1977 Quality of Employment Survey* (Ann Arbor: University of Michigan Survey Research Center, 1979), p. 306; employment growth data from U.S. Bureau of Labor Statistics.

historically have enjoyed above-average levels of work satisfaction, while clerical and service workers have been relatively dissatisfied with their jobs. Occupations representing a dwindling share of national employment demonstrate a similar ambiguity—laborers and unskilled workers have always expressed considerable dissatisfaction with their work, but farmers have consistently registered the highest contentment of any occupational category. On balance, the growth of professional/management roles and the decline in unskilled laborers probably are of greater significance than less promising trends, but the implications for overall job satisfaction are far from clear.

A more sophisticated way of evaluating changes in the nature of work is to look directly at shifts in aggregate job skill requirements over time. To avoid the vague assumptions implicit in the use of broad occupational categories, it is necessary to assess the combined effect of shifts in overall occupational distribution and in skill levels of specific occupations on aggregate job skill requirements. Following this approach, one study suggests that the distribution of skill requirements narrowed between 1960 and 1976—both low-skilled and high-skilled jobs dwindled in this period, while those with moderate skill requirements increased.[3] Some unskilled positions have disappeared, enhancing the potential for satisfying work, but work roles have not uniformly improved and the loss of high-skilled positions may clash sharply with rising expectations and education levels in the workforce.

The evidence of occupational shifts or fluctuations in skill levels fails to support claims of uniform improvements or deterioration in work quality. The economy has continued to generate stifling and menial work: in the four largest expanding occupational groups (secretaries, of whom there are 5.0 million; food service, 4.4 million; retail clerks, 3.1 million; drivers and delivery, 2.9 million), there are neither signs of rapid change nor hopes of immediate advances in work quality. Some jobs are now cleaner, safer or more interesting, but others offer less freedom and require fewer skills. In this sense, accounts of the demise of blue-collar work or the emergence of a service economy are misleading—they usually imply improvements in the quality of work or the potential for job satisfaction. A more realistic view recognizes that there is more continuity than change in the labor market, and that white-collar or service jobs are not necessarily "better" in offering hope for work satisfaction.

Technology: Threat or Panacea?

If there is a driving force behind occupational change, it lies in the continuing process of technological innovation. From the invention of the wheel to the introduction of the computer, technological change has shaped the structure and content of work, moving the labor force from farm to factory to office. Invariably, the prospect of rapid technological advance has generated both hopes and fears—ranging from utopian visions of a workless society to modern-day Luddites who bemoan the potential loss of skills and displacement of workers. Even as the process of technological innovation generates steadily-rising levels of societal affluence, the debate over the impact of new technologies on work quality and the potential for job satisfaction persists.

During the 1960s and early 1970s, the prophecies of "technological optimists" abounded. Technology, many believed, would free workers in fully automated plants from their former bondage to machines. Fewer workers would monitor the operations, and their direct control of the processes would relieve the burden of rigid, repetitive operations and close supervision typical in machine-paced, mass-production industries. More responsible, highly trained individuals would be employed at broader, more rewarding tasks, and automation would make the factory cleaner, safer and more challenging. In this view, blue-collar work would tend to become "white-coated" if not white-collared, and implicitly more varied and creative as well.

No doubt, part of this rose-colored vision has indeed been realized. Present-day workplaces are better designed for safety and comfort, and automated technologies—especially in the steel, construction and mining industries—has sharply reduced requirements for physical labor. Yet the promise of a new day for blue-collar work in terms of skill, challenge and interest is far from having been realized. As previously discussed, skill levels in the labor market have not uniformly improved, and the automation of industrial processes has even decreased opportunities for creative work in some settings. While challenges in the design stages of new processes or products have expanded, required skills are usually mechanized at the manufacturing stage for maximum efficiency and production jobs rarely emerge improved. The efficient manufacture of standardized products simply has not lent itself to jobs which are variable, creative, or demanding of high skill levels.

In the meantime, however, the terms of the debate have also changed. As recently as in the early 1970s, the prospects of a dramatically new type of technology were not as apparent as they are a mere decade later. Rather than anticipating incremental advances, futurists are increasingly discussing the onset of a sweeping technological revolution, one which would rival or surpass the Industrial Revolution of the 19th century in importance. Although the new social order which is envisioned has been given many names—"postindustrial," "technetronic" or "information" society—the sense of impending transformation as a result of technological change has come to dominate discussions of the future of work. Any view of approaching changes in work quality or job satisfaction rests (consciously or otherwise) on judgments of the strength of this claim that a technological revolution is in the offing.

Silicon Chips and Robots

At the center of this flurry of interest in technological change is the microprocessor. While computer technology has made widespread automation theoretically feasible for more than a decade, barriers of size and cost have blocked the economical application of computer capabilities in most work settings. Large and expensive computer systems could produce cost savings only in the most massive industrial settings, and automated machinery could not be easily adapted to serve various production functions. Yet, with the development of the microprocessor, these obstacles have been overcome and the potential uses of computerized machinery at the workplace have dramatically increased.

Microprocessor technology is best symbolized by the silicon chip, a miniaturized system of integrated circuits which can direct electrical current and thereby generate vast computational power. With current technology, a silicon chip the size of one square centimeter can perform millions of multiplications per second, and has the capacity to store the complete texts of the Declaration of Independence, the Constitution, and a few chapters of the Federalist Papers. Technological advances are expected to result in at least a fourfold expansion of these capabilities within a decade, so that the microprocessors of the future will be extremely powerful computers on a single silicon chip or combination of chips. The reduction is size is astounding—today's hand-held programmable calculators have more computational power than the first full-scale computers built during World War II, computers which could have been "hand held" only by juggling 18,000 different vacuum tubes.

This unprecedented miniaturization of computer technology is particularly important because it has been accompanied by dramatic cost reductions, making microprocessors economically competitive in a wide range of industrial applications. Once designed, silicon chips can be mass produced at a very low cost, and even further price declines are anticipated as volumes rise. As a result, a calculation which cost 80 cents to perform in the early 1950s now costs less than one cent, after adjusting for inflation. The combined reductions in size and cost of microprocessor technology have triggered renewed interest in prospects for automation and in the broader possibility of a wholesale transformation of modern society driven by these new technological capabilities.

The silicon chip is particularly important to economical automation because it provides the basis for fully integrating computer and machine. In industrial settings, the microprocessor makes possible the development of manufacturing machinery with unique adaptability. One author observed:

> This flexibility is of fundamental importance. Until now, automation has been largely restricted to factories that turn out thousands of identical products, because it has been too costly to retool machines at frequent intervals to perform new tasks. But the development of reprogrammable machinery makes it economically feasible to automate production processes that involve short

production-runs and frequent changes in machine settings.[4]

The great majority—at least 75 percent—of all manufactured goods fall into the category of shorter, lower-volume production runs, with only the most basic industries continuing to fit the mass-production stereotype. Technological advances in microelectronics, therefore, were an essential precondition to widespread automation, and the expanding use of reprogrammable machinery has triggered today's intense debate regarding the future of industrialized societies.

The potential impact of microprocessors is heightened by their seemingly endless number of applications. This new technology promises to alter not only the factory, but the office as well. Sophisticated word processors and computerized information storage and retrieval systems are becoming increasingly cost-effective, and because this new technology does not require knowledge of specialized computer languages, their growing use may raise traditionally low productivity among office workers. As in the case of factory technologies, these office innovations are seen by many as qualitatively different from previous office equipment which "mechanized" or "automated" routine tasks—for example, an American association of office workers views microprocessor technology as a dramatic new force "because the new technology is being developed to computerize the very flow of work in the office."[5] While memory typewriters made an office worker's tasks easier, emerging computer technologies may change the means by which information is transcribed and made available to others. Again, only with the silicon chip has this decentralized use of computer technology at affordable cost become possible.

The use of the microprocessor to automate production functions is epitomized by the development of the robot. Prior to the last decade, robots were confined to the domain of children's stories and science fiction—their practical and efficient application in work settings was virtually inconceivable given the state of computer technology. Yet the silicon chip has thrust robots from fantasy to reality, and the technology is being pursued with remarkable speed and vigor. A number of top computer companies are now considering entry into the robot market, and several large U.S. corporations have made major commitments to purchase robots which are already available. The use of robots in manufacturing has nearly quadrupled in a mere two years between 1979 and 1981, and most analysts expect the sales curve to shoot even higher during the next few years.[6] Most importantly, microprocessors seem to be in a prime position for the implementation of "learning curve pricing" strategies in which firms lower prices in anticipation of rising volumes and declining unit costs. The entry of large computer companies into the robot market could ensure this aggressive marketing stance and trigger a sharp rise in robot sales by 1990.

Today's robots bear little resemblance to the creations of screenplay writers and science fiction authors. Rather than being a form of mechanical humanoid, industrial robots are characterized by mechanical arms linked to reprogrammable computers. An exact definition of a robot, as distinct from other automated machinery, eludes even industry representatives; the Robot Institute of America, an industrial trade group, stresses that it is the "reprogrammable and multifunctional" character of robots which is unique, allowing them to perform a variety of tasks.[7] And the emerging versions of robots certainly are varied—the more extravagant include a "bureaucratic robot" which stamps signatures on letters, a robot "nurse" to assist people in wheelchairs, a robot "janitor and guard dog" for the home, and "talking robots" which would advertise products or give job training to illiterates. In other fields of endeavor, microprocessors are revolutionizing design methods for the development of new manufactured goods, and have become an integral part of nearly all modern research equipment so as to expedite lengthy data analysis.[8] Innovations such as voice-sensitive computers which can directly transcribe dictation into written text may be marketable within just a few years.

"I think we've taken this robot business too far!"

It is this overwhelming diversity of applications for microprocessor technology which distinguishes it from less significant innovations and which has led futurists to predict a societal transformation "comparable with the agricultural revolution that began about 10,000 years ago and with the industrial revolution."[9] Yet many of these same authors provide no sense of the nature of work in such a "postindustrial" society. Will microprocessors bring a wave of automation so sweeping as to leave millions without meaningful work roles? If new jobs are created to replace those lost through automation, will they provide more or less satisfaction to workers? And finally, if we are in the midst of a broad transformation of the workplace, how will we cope with the displacement of workers caught in the transition?

These fundamental questions cannot be ignored amidst rapid technological advance.

Will Robots Make Us Obsolete?

There is little consensus as to where the "robot revolution" is heading and how far it will go. The technology itself may be refined to such an extent that most factory work could be carried out by robots and automated machinery—for example, a study conducted at Carnegie-Mellon University asserts that the current generation of robots has the technical capability to perform nearly 7 million existing factory jobs—one-third of all manufacturing employment—and that sometime after 1990 it will become technically possible to replace all manufacturing operatives in the automotive, electrical equipment, machinery and fabricated metals industries.[10] Yet these theoretical estimates of the potential for automation, which reach as high as 65 to 75 percent of the factory workforce, do not reflect the rate at which the new technology will actually be introduced to the workplace. The pace of innovation will depend on the relative costs of labor and computerized technologies, as well as on broader levels of supply and demand for goods and services. Predictions of this nature are infinitely more difficult than abstract assessments of future technological capabilities.

The automobile industry offers an interesting case study, because it is probably the first manufacturing industry to aggressively pursue the use of robots in automated processes. The push toward automation in the auto industry is a response to both rising labor costs and growing concerns for quality control and competitiveness in international markets. As Senator Lloyd Bentsen recently noted, auto manufacturers already find it possible to operate robots for $6 per hour, well below the $20 per hour required for the pay and benefits of a skilled worker.[11] With an awareness of the growing use of robots by Japanese auto makers, General

Motors now predicts that by 1987, 90 percent of all its new capital investments will be in computer-controlled machines.[12] A 1980 survey conducted by the American Society of Manufacturing Engineers predicted that robots will replace 20 percent of existing jobs in the auto industry by 1985, and that 50 percent of automobile assembly will be done by automated machines (including robots) by 1995.[13] Even the United Auto Workers anticipates a 20 percent decline in membership by 1990 and has successfully obtained advance notice and retraining rights from auto manufacturers in a growing effort to gain protection from sweeping automation. Yet few of these estimates include any consideration of the extent to which capital shortages confronting robot manufacturers and purchasers may limit the speed with which the new technology is adopted.

Projections of the impact of microprocessors on office employment are even more problematic, with analysts more frequently predicting the number of office jobs "affected" rather than eliminated by automation. The Carnegie-Mellon study argued that 38 million of 50 million existing white-collar jobs would eventually be affected by automation, while a vice president for strategic planning for Xerox Corporation offered the more conservative guess of 20-30 million jobs affected by 1990 (Table 5-2).[14] There is a general recognition that office technologies will be changing rapidly, but little sense of whether the result will be reduced office employment, shifts in future employment growth, or simply higher levels of productivity in white-collar settings.

A 1981 study prepared for the International Labour Office found that microelectronic technology has not caused widespread displacement of office workers, but perhaps only because of the impact of poor economic conditions on the rate of diffusion of the new technology in office settings. Selected case studies of the banking and insurance industries suggested that new job opportunities were being created, but that the skills made redundant by new technologies were

Table 5-2 Robots and Computers Will Affect Workers in Both Factories and Offices

In factories	Number of employees
Assemblers	1,289,000
Checkers, examiners, inspectors, testers	746,000
Production painters	185,000
Welders and flame-cutters	713,000
Packagers	626,000
Machiner operatives	2,385,000
Other skilled workers	1,043,000
Total	6,987,000

In offices	Number of employees
Managers	9,000,000
Other professionals	14,000,000
Secretaries and support workers	5,000,000
Clerks	10,000,000
Total	38,000,000

Source: *The Impacts on the Workforce & Workplace,* Carnegie-Mellon University; Booz, Allen & Hamilton, Inc.

generally inappropriate for those emerging opportunities. The ILO report stressed that this trend poses special threats to future employment prospects for women, and called for additional education and training efforts to close the "skill gap" caused by the use of microprocessors in office jobs.[15]

Perhaps the greatest fears that automation will lead to widespread unemployment have been voiced, not in the United States, but in Western Europe. For example, two British authors have predicted nothing short of the collapse of work as a social institution in an era of microprocessors, writing:

> It is impossible to over-dramatize the forthcoming crisis as it potentially strikes a blow at the very core of industrialized societies—the work ethic. We have based our social structures on this ethic and now it would appear that it is to become redundant along with millions of other people.[16]

In West Germany, studies of the impact of automation on future employment levels commissioned by the Bonn government projected that the number of jobs in 1990 will at best be marginally above 1977 levels—a pessimistic view in light of anticipated population growth. The issue of technologically induced unemployment increasingly is capturing the attention of West European leaders, and unions in Italy, Germany and elsewhere are responding with demands for shorter workweeks to protect employment levels. Perennial fears that machines would replace men have never been fulfilled, but European futurists insist that it will be different this time.

The distinction between the "robotic revolution" and earlier waves of technological innovation is not devoid of rationality. While the impact of automation in the past has been offset by the emergence of new industries and by growth in the service sector of the economy, these avenues for employment growth may indeed be less open in an era of microprocessors. The electronics industry which supports this computerized technology certainly will experience rapid growth in the coming decade, but a 1979 survey of the world electronics industry prepared for the Organization for Economic Cooperation and Development revealed that the internal use of its own technology will keep employment growth in this sector to a minimum.[17] It is this "reproductive" potential of computerized technology—the prospect of robots building robots—which challenges traditional patterns of employment growth through new industries. And to the extent that the microprocessor will affect service as well as manufacturing industries, even the recent trend of expanding service employment may fail to provide jobs for all who seek them.

In spite of these relatively unique characteristics of microprocessor applications, predictions of immediate and massive job losses tend to ignore the market forces which slow the pace of technological change. As stressed in recent research by the Bureau of Labor Statistics, many factors limit the speed of diffusion of technological change and thereby mitigate possible employment implications. The size of required investment, the rate of capacity utilization and the institutional arrangements within industries all can act as "economic governors" which slow the adoption of automated technologies.[18]

Virtually all capital-intensive industries have a massive investment in existing plant facilities, and they cannot afford to squander these resources through the wholesale replacement of working machinery. More importantly, the financial constraints on capital formation necessarily limit the rate at which new technologies are introduced. In this context, Joseph Engleberger, president of Unimation, Inc. (the nation's largest robot manufacturer), has dismissed predictions of galloping automation, noting that even the replacement of 5 percent of all blue-collar workers in Western industrialized nations would require investments totalling $3 billion in each of the next 40 years.[19] While microprocessor technology may be promising in its flexibility and potential efficiency, industries must be able to afford the new acquisitions in order to use them.

A less tangible but perhaps equally important force limiting the expansion of computer technology lies in the attitudes of both workers and consumers. While a computer may be able to diagnose medical problems, its bedside manner may be less than comforting. Similarly, word processors and telephone answering systems may alter clerical roles, but most executives will not want to forego the convenience offered by their personal secretaries. Even on the assembly line, where robots may be perfectly suited for production processes, the aversion of managers and workers to such unfamiliar companions may hamper their smooth and rapid assimilation at the workplace. These psychological barriers cannot be factored into equations of economic efficiency, but they are likely to slow the pace of technological change nonetheless.

The picture which emerges when the functioning of capital markets and work organizations are considered is one of evolutionary rather than revolutionary change. With annual sales of robots well below even a figure as modest as 10,000 in an economy supporting a labor force of more than 100 million, it will be some time before computerized technologies make a major dent in aggregate employment levels. This perspective is emphasized by Robotics International, a professional group which polled 100 users and manufacturers of robots. Based on the responses, the group concluded that robots are likely to replace 440,000 rather than a million workers by 1990, and that all but 5 percent of those would be retrained rather than dismissed.[20] The relative lack of union concern in the United States over aggregate job losses through automation also stems from this belief that the pace of innovation has been exaggerated. William Winpisinger, president of the International Association of Machinists, has argued that the replacement of human skills with computerized machinery will occur slowly and that a shortage of skilled workers will remain our most pressing manpower problem.[21] No doubt guarantees of job security will continue to be sought in some industries and collective bargaining may gradually extend to include management investment decisions, but the workplace will not be transformed overnight.

In the more distant future, no one can be sure where new employment growth will occur. Expectations of a workless society still linger; as described in one forecast:

> Earning a living may no longer be a necessity but a privilege; services may have to be protected from automation, and given certain social status; leisure time activities may have to be invented in order to give new meaning to a mode of life that may have become economically useless for a majority of the populace.[22]

The literature in recent decades has been replete with speculations on how people would cope with the loss of meaningful work roles, or how society would allocate and distribute wealth in the absence of strong ties between work and income.[23] Even for those who reject such forebodings, the belief in continued employment growth admittedly contains as much faith as foresight.

Still, there seems little likelihood that the worker will become obsolete in the foreseeable future. In one sense, past waves of automation have created dislocations, but these have been distributed throughout the labor force in the form of benefits and social progress—shorter workweeks, more vacation time, longer training and education, earlier retirement, child labor laws, and welfare and unemployment payments. We can expect this trend to continue, particularly as labor seeks assurances of job security. Assuming a healthy rate of economic growth during a period of innovation and increasing automation, it is also likely that levels of aggregate demand will support the emergence of new goods and services, including some presently beyond imagination. Rising expectations alone will cause Americans to translate productivity gains into higher standards of living instead of less work, a pattern which has held for centuries. The period of adjustment which lies ahead may not be painless, but it seems that work is here to stay. And we might add hurrah to that prediction.

Work Quality Amidst Automation

If people continue to spend a substantial portion of their waking hours at work, will they find work amidst robots and computers significantly different and less satisfying? The answer depends largely on the extent to which specific technologies leave room for challenging human tasks. It does not appear that automation will have a uniform impact on the quality of work. The worst jobs may disappear as robots march into factories, but workers may find as much to complain about in their new computerized world.

The promising aspects of microprocessor technology are certainly significant. Robots usually assume the most dangerous and unpleasant work tasks, including those involving hazardous substances, heavy materials and repetitive functions. Computerized technology can create the potential for significant job upgrading as well, freeing workers from mundane responsibilities and allowing them to take on more challenging roles. In industrial settings, automation can provide workers with greater freedom at the workplace, particularly allowing a kind of physical mobility seldom possible in more traditional assembly-line factories. Finally, new technologies—whether word processors or sophisticated manufacturing tools—can enhance workers' sense of power, allowing them to master more complex machinery and feel more productive or effective in their jobs.

These gains in potential satisfaction will not occur automatically. Many of the improvements in work quality are as much a function of management decisions as of the new technologies, and automation can as easily produce work situations which are worse instead of better. Button pushing and machine watching, like bolt tightening, hardly lift the spirit or challenge the intellect. Automated systems can decrease the importance of human talents, placing the "skill" in the machine as part of efforts to control and standardize quality. Computerized technologies also give managers and supervisors greater ability to monitor worker performance, thereby increasing job pressures and the potential for work dissatisfaction. While improving worker safety, automation can create totally new health hazards (e.g., eye strain and nerve disorders caused by computer terminals). Finally, the basic insecurities aroused by change, by the lack of familiarity with new and complex equipment, provide a source of psychological discomfort for workers, especially in their later years. To the extent that stability and knowledge engender feelings of control and satisfaction, even generally positive innovations can undermine subjective perceptions of work quality.

Without question, the most serious threat to work satisfaction posed by the age of robots and microprocessors is the prospect of growing disparities between worker skills and labor market demands. The total number of jobs may not diminish, but it seems increasingly likely that the skills of workers in declining industries will be poorly suited to the manpower requirements of new growth sectors. Those displaced workers who are fortunate enough to find work in growth industries may discover that their interests and talents are not easily adapted to their new work roles, leaving them feeling overwhelmed and incompetent. And the less fortunate may become little more than relics of a past era, accepting jobs which represent the dregs of the labor market or falling victim to the plight of the structurally unemployed. Virtually all contemporary reviews of robotics and automation make at least passing reference to the problem of worker displacement, and call for innovative training efforts to cushion the impact of technological change.

The severity of the worker displacement problem will depend partially on future trends in productivity and employment growth. Thus far, labor unions have sought guarantees of retraining and placement in new jobs for workers displaced by automated technologies, and the numbers have been small enough that companies such as General Electric have been able to observe a no-layoff policy without incurring unacceptable costs. However, as the pace of innovation accelerates and in the absence of significant jumps in productivity, this appeasement of union concerns may become considerably less palatable; management typically justifies the capital costs of automation by citing reduced labor costs, and labor demands for job security are fundamentally at odds with that result. As robots move into more attractive jobs, the potential for conflict over automation can only escalate.

Organized labor may find that it has more at stake than merely the job security of its members. Automated technologies can eventually undermine the leverage and power of unions, permitting aspects of production to proceed during labor disputes with minimal supervision by management personnel. More importantly, union participation in decisions concerning the use of new technologies may be the only way to ensure that automation offers protection to displaced workers and to prevent increasing hierarchical control and supervision over workers. Geographic shifts of high technology to the Sunbelt region where unions are weakest will further aggravate the problems of displaced workers as they cope with technological change. These issues surely will test the stength of organized labor in sectors of rapid innovation and declining employment.

Perhaps most discouraging is the realization that, even if union efforts to ensure worker retraining are successful, automation may spell trouble for new, unskilled entrants to the labor market. By seeking to avoid layoffs, prospects for job creation and the training of inexperienced workers in automating industries are diminished—simply stated, "Young people with limited skills are likely to find it harder to get work in an automated society if new jobs are preferentially given to those who have become redundant."[24] Again, there is reason to believe that new areas of employment growth will emerge to dispel fears of widespread unemployment. Yet the problems of teenagers and other unskilled labor force participants, already growing serious in the United States, may suffer from relative neglect as policymakers focus attention on the needs of workers displaced by new technologies.

In summary, robots do not portend disaster for labor market operations. Their introduction will be relatively slow, and most of their early tasks will be cheerfully forsaken by labor. Much of the subsequent impact of automation on the quality of work will depend on the success of workers in obtaining a voice in the introduction and control of new technologies—robots and computers will not necessarily diminish job satisfaction, but they increasingly will provide the context for labor-management battles over the quality of work. Adjusting to the age of robots and computer technology in a way which meets the needs of displaced workers must be a first priority as this debate continues.

The Challenge of Adjustment

Even assuming that changes in the nature of work do not negate the prospects for job satisfaction among tomorrow's workers, they do threaten to wreak havoc upon today's labor force participants who may be caught in their path. Both current occupational shifts and the technological changes by which they are driven necessarily eliminate the work roles of thousands of Americans, many of whom are ill prepared for the transition to new jobs. The ordeal of change, to borrow Eric Hoffer's phrase, is inherent in the continuing evolution of work, and yet the adjustments to current changes in the workplace may be especially difficult due to the scope of technological change. While the quality and availability of work may not suffer in the transition, a sizable portion of the modern labor force certainly will.

Some of the reasons why the challenge of adjustment looms so large have already been discussed. In our "information society," knowledge of innovations spreads throughout the labor market with unprecedented speed, so that shifts in both the demand for labor and the technology of the workplace have accelerated. In addition, the nature of technological change now is distinctly different from prior eras as the microprocessor is altering work processes in a wide range of manufacturing and service industries. Workers with few intellectual and technical skills necessary for successful adaptation are particularly vulnerable; the changes threaten their very livelihood and tend to diminish their prospects for satisfaction at the workplace.

Yet the transitional problems facing the contemporary labor force are also exacerbated by the growing size and interdependence of today's markets. With dramatic advances in transportation and communication technologies during the past few decades, the world has become a much smaller place and individual communities or even nations have lost some measure of control over their own destinies. The erosion of blue-collar work in declining manufacturing industries is a reflection not only of technological innovation and shifts in aggregate demand, but also of the inability of American industries to compete in international markets for the production of durable goods. International trade has become an increasingly important part of the American economy, growing dramatically as a share of our GNP in recent years. This movement toward a world economy will continue to reshape the structure of domestic industries, and will restrict the ability of national public policy to control or limit change in the domestic labor market.

Examples of work trends driven by forces of international competition are plentiful. Employment in the American automobile and steel industries has fallen steadily because domestic manufacturers have been increasingly unable to compete with foreign producers. Similarly, even if we were to conclude as a nation that the use of robots would diminish unacceptably the quality of work, it would prove virtually impossible to ban them from American workplaces and still protect employment levels in the face of foreign competition. Our rising levels of wages and societal affluence have given us a comparative advantage in the production of high technology goods and the delivery of sophisticated services, while at the same time leaving us less and less able to produce labor-intensive durable goods at favorable prices. In all of these areas, any attempt to halt patterns of occupational and technological change not only would impose costs through a reduced standard of living but would also jeopardize the very employment it was intended to preserve by undermining our international competitiveness.

Thus, our options for responding to the problems of displaced workers have become narrower, at least in terms of the ability of unions or government to maintain artificially high employment levels within given industries. The only rational and appropriate course for public policy in responding to the challenges of adjustment is to attempt to facilitate and accelerate the transition for workers themselves—through retraining and placement efforts rather than through trade barriers and protections for declining industries. This approach certainly has not yet been embraced by the Reagan administration, which continues to hope that economic growth will somehow relieve the strains of adjustment facing displaced workers. Unfortunately, if more direct assistance is not provided to those affected by occupational shifts and technological change, the price of progress in terms of work opportunity and satisfaction will remain frightfully high.

6 A Portrait of Tomorrow's Worker

> Every man's work, whether it be
> literature or music or pictures
> or architecture or anything else,
> is always a portrait of himself.
>
> —Samuel Butler
> *The Way of All Flesh*

As the content of work changes, the characteristics of those who hold jobs and the hopes and expectations which they bring to the workplace also undergo constant revision. We often refer to "rewarding jobs" as though every task offered some predetermined level of fulfillment, and yet work satisfaction is inherently subjective in nature. For this reason, the evolution of the labor force cannot be ignored in gauging the likelihood of future contentment at work.

Past trends demonstrate that job satisfaction is neither objective nor absolute. In any objective sense, the quality of work has improved considerably in recent decades—real wages have risen dramatically, considerable gains in worker health and safety have been achieved, and the proportion of the labor force in skilled or professional roles has steadily increased. Nonetheless, by all available measures, overall job satisfaction among workers has remained constant, with worker expectations rising at least as fast as tangible work gains. What constitutes "good pay" or "dignifying work" changes over time, and the yardstick by which we measure work quality gradually lengthens. Today's job may have been yesterday's wildest dream, but there is no guarantee that tomorrow's worker will be satisfied with it.

The composition of the workforce serves as an important variable in the job satisfaction equation. The educational attainment and affluence of labor force participants, as well as their age, sex and race, all affect their expectations at the workplace and their aspirations for future jobs. These characteristics of the American workforce have changed significantly in recent decades, with workers becoming increasingly educated, affluent, young and female. When compared to changes in the nature of work itself, the implications of these trends for potential job satisfaction seem more predictable and at least as important.

The Educated Workforce

While today's workers may not be brighter than their predecessors, they certainly bring longer schooling to the workplace. Through major public investments in a comprehensive educational system spanning from kindergarten to postgraduate programs, the United States has achieved impressive advances toward the goal of a universally educated population. The median educational attainment of 8.7 years that a worker brought to the job in 1940 rose in four decades to 12.7 years (Figure 6.1). The greatest gains in education have accrued to those who formerly had the least schooling, and the segment of the labor force with less than three years of high school is expected to continue its sharp decline throughout the 1980s.

Typically, we view education as an unqualified good, and from a societal viewpoint these rising education levels may indeed bode well for our cultural development and for the vitality of our democratic system—at least that's the hope. Yet in a narrower sense, more schooling does not necessarily foster greater contentment among workers. As Americans in all occupations enter the labor market with more education than ever before, the prospect of educational gains outpacing skill requirements becomes more threatening. If the rising educational attainment of workers was accompanied by an increase in the number of demanding and challenging jobs, there would be cause for optimism. Unfortunately, the evidence suggests that the extra certificates and diplomas may produce little more for modern workers than higher goals and more frequent disappointments.

Before World War II, employers had few formal entry requirements—employees needed only some basic reading and writing skills and elementary mastery of ciphers to qualify for most jobs. Wartime production did increase the demand for technical and craft skills, and the subsequent eras of computers and microprocessors have maintained requirements for specialized training in fields of rapid technological advance. However, most of the increase in education levels has occurred independently of the technical

124

Figure 6.1 Educational Attainments of the Labor Force Have Grown Steadily

Percent

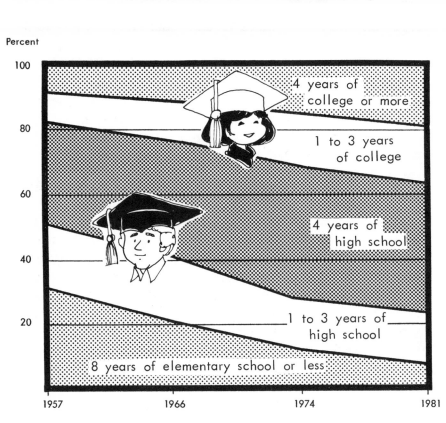

Source: U.S. Bureau of Labor Statistics, *Educational Attainment of Workers, March 1979,* Special Labor Force Report 240 (Washington: U.S. Government Printing Office, 1981), p. A-9.

requirements of the labor market, with more highly educated workers performing essentially the same functions as their less schooled predecessors. During the 1970s, the portion of professional and technical workers who were college graduates rose from 61 to 71 percent among men and from 54 to 63 percent among women. The share of sales and clerical workers with college degrees nearly doubled in the course of that decade, as did the percentage of blue-collar and service workers with one or more years of college.[1] With one of every five salespersons college-educated, it is difficult to interpret further gains in formal education as a response to skill requirements in the labor market.

There are rational explanations for the continuing rise in educational attainment. For the individual worker, education continues to pay off. Estimates prepared by the Bureau of the Census (adjusted for 1981 dollars) indicate that a worker with only 8 years of education could anticipate lifetime earnings of $850,000; in contrast, workers with 12 years of education can hope for $1.2 million, those with 16 years can anticipate $1.8 million, and those with 17 or more years of schooling will earn an estimated $2.1 million during their lifetimes. The income advantage enjoyed by college graduates is not as great as it used to be—as colleges and universities award increasing numbers of degrees, the relative pecuniary worth of a sheepskin declines. Yet it still makes sense from an individual's perspective to seek a college education, for it broadens employment options and enhances personal earning potential.

The uncertainties of the hiring process add to the incentives for furthering one's education. Employers frequently rely upon formal education as a screening device, using these credentials to rationalize the allocation of jobs even when the work itself does not require the added training. Thus, if a college and a high school graduate compete for the same position, an employer usually will hire the former because that person is "better qualified"—a strength not necessarily related to the ability to perform required job tasks in a satisfactory manner. This screening activity becomes particularly pronounced during periods of high unemployment, when college-educated workers are more likely to accept positions for which they are "overeducated" as a preferable alternative to joblessness. The rise in educational attainment eventually creates a spiral which builds on itself. The growing number of college graduates forces others to seek higher education in order to compete for scarce jobs, and the average education level among workers creeps upward, even if the labor market does not require the added investment in education.

More education is a response to the threat of unemployment in another sense—as previously mentioned, extended education is one of the ways in which society "allocates" or "distributes" joblessness. By absorbing large numbers of young people, institutions of higher education delay their entry into the labor force and provide an "aging vat" which prevents further strains in the labor market. Along with the armed forces, colleges and universities offer a socially accepted alternative to unemployment, one which public policy actively encourages and financially supports. The maturation of the "baby-boom" generation and the rise in college enrollments during the late 1960s and early 1970s were hardly coincidental, but rather a predictable response to a labor surplus. While tighter labor markets in the future would increase the attractiveness of work as opposed to longer schooling, the recent inability of the economy to generate an adequate supply of jobs for youthful workers suggests that higher education will continue to provide a useful "holding tank" for both the individual and society.

Were it not for the expectations engendered by higher education, the increasing diversion of our youth to colleges and universities might offer an ideal way of coping with insufficient aggregate employment. Yet more schooling invariably raises hopes of higher earnings and greater career advancement, setting the stage for worker disillusionment and discontent should labor market opportunities lag behind such expectations. Job satisfaction surveys have identified the combination of longer schooling and low pay as one of the most potent formulas for dissatisfaction at the workplace, reflecting the belief education credentials implicitly promise or guarantee future success. In sending them to school for longer stints, we prepare a veritable "powder keg" of expectations among new entrants to the labor force, who by virtue of youth and inexperience are the most likely to suffer from the inadequacies of the labor market.

Signs that labor market requirements have not kept pace with the expectations of an educated workforce abound. In a landmark study, Ivar Berg estimated that in 1970, one-fifth of all college graduates held jobs which did not require their level of educational attainment.[2] Workers' own assessments of the match between their academic credentials and actual job requirements have reinforced that finding; the University of Michigan's 1970 *Survey of Working Conditions* found that more than one in three workers believed they had more education than their jobs required.[3] Finally, the data on initial job placements of college graduates in more recent years suggest that the correlation between educational attainment and jobs has not improved—almost 90 percent of college graduates entering the labor force between 1962 and 1969 assumed professional, technical, managerial or administrative roles, while less than two-thirds of those entering between 1969 and 1976 succeeded in obtaining similar positions (Table 6-1).

The potential for a growing mismatch between skill requirements and workers' educational attainment is a source of increasing concern among labor market analysts. According to one estimate, college graduates entering the labor force are likely to exceed job openings in professional and managerial categories by some 2.7 million over the next decade, leaving 2.5 graduates to compete for every choice job.[4] A detailed study of changes in general skill requirements and educational attainment among workers during the period from 1960 to 1976 confirmed that the incidence of overeducation in the labor market had increased.[5] With employment growth likely to occur primarily in low-skilled clerical, retail trade and service jobs, this pattern of widening disparities between job opportunities, educational attainment and worker expectations seems certain to persist.

Table 6-1
Between 1962 and 1969, Four Million College Graduates Entered the Labor Force Compared with Eight Million Graduates During the Succeeding Seven Years

	1962-1969	1969-1976
Professional and technical	72.6%	46.1%
Management and administration	17.1	18.4
Sales	2.9	8.4
Clerical	3.0	10.5
Craft	2.5	3.1
Operatives	0.5	2.0
Nonfarm laborers	0.1	1.0
Service	0.5	4.6
Farm workers	0.2	1.2
Unemployed	0.1	4.7

Source: "Entry Jobs for College Graduates: The Occupational Mix is Changing," *Monthly Labor Review,* June 1978, p. 52.

The problems arising from the overeducation of the workforce are not easily catalogued, but the possibilities are disturbing. Worker dissatisfaction with jobs which fail to utilize this education is the most obvious of possible results. Yet the consequences of a mismatch between education and jobs may reach much farther to include deteriorating mental and physical health, falling productivity, and rising frequency of disruptive behavior among workers. The current trends in turnover, absenteeeism, and other outward manifestations of worker attitudes are as yet unconvincing in this regard, but our apparent inability to provide suitable opportunities for more educated workers must be a source of serious concern. Collectively at least, we may not be doing our children any favors by sending them off to college and graduate school unless labor market conditions improve in the years ahead.

How much we as a society should invest in education remains a normative decision—one based more on the value we place on an educated populace than on narrow measures of the economic returns reaped from more schooling. In this sense, it is possible that we can never have an "overeducated" workforce, that the concept by definition ignores the presumed societal benefits of universal education. Yet we must still address the possibility of rising dissatisfaction at the workplace which has led a major union leader to conclude, "America has to start worrying about turning out Ph.D.s who end up as cab drivers and start training for the kind of jobs that are really needed in society."[6] If, as critics charge, higher education is becoming nothing more than longer education providing few skills and opening few occupational doors, it should not be surprising to find our more educated workers less satisfied with the jobs in which they are eventually placed.

Having More and Expecting More

Along with the educational upgrading of the nation's workforce, growing affluence has had an equally pervasive influence on work attitudes. By impressive margins, American workers have more money than ever before, and until the mid-1970s, this relative personal wealth continued its steady upward climb. For nearly three decades following World War II, average real wages moved upward in an unbroken record of annual gains. Even the disastrous setbacks of the 1930s only arrested temporarily the growth of real personal income, but failed to alter the long term pattern of improved economic status of employed workers (Figure 6.2). While these average real wage increases have not solved the problems of relative poverty and unequal distribution of wealth, they have represented great gains for the majority of workers.

Figure 6.2   Average Annual Compensation Per Full Time Equivalent Employee Rose Steadily Until the Mid-1970s

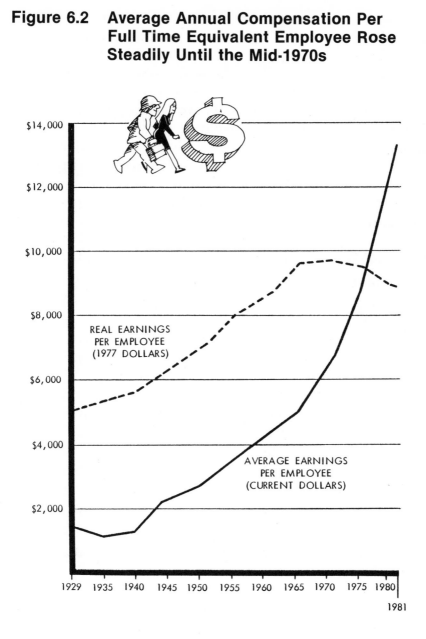

Source: Bureau of Economic Analysis, U.S. Department of Commerce.

These income gains alter the nature of worker expectations and demands on the job. At least some workers begin to climb Maslow's needs hierarchy (assuming that it exists), satisfying to a large extent the more basic needs that good pay can fulfill and moving on to seek "higher-order" social and psychological rewards at the workplace. While financial compensation remains important to most workers, it is more easily taken for granted in an affluent era. Real incomes which would have seemed like a king's ransom fifty years ago now are accepted as a matter or course, and in themselves are sometimes insufficient inducements for lasting job attachment.

Attitude Changes Magnified by Youth

In addition to bringing higher expectations to the workplace, more affluent workers have a greater number of options with regard to work. They are better able to assume the risks of rejecting their current jobs; particularly as the number of two-income households swells, it becomes easier for workers to bear the costs of job transitions. Workers with higher real incomes are also able to trade income gains for leisure, taking longer weekends and vacations to escape from unpleasant jobs. Thus, even if levels of worker dissatisfaction have not increased in recent years, it is more likely that today's workers will act upon their feelings of discontent.

By the early 1970s, the prolonged rise of real incomes had visibly altered worker attitudes. Young workers were part of a generation untempered by the fire of mass unemployment and falling wages, and they were more likely to risk the displeasure of their employers because they assumed other work would be available at the same or better wages. When the automobile industry was booming, the story was told of a young autoworker who, although usually a model employee, never appeared for work on Fridays. He was finally accosted by his supervisor, and explained his habit of working only four days a week with the reply, "I don't make enough to live on three day's wages." Although this defiant attitude would take more courage amidst the layoffs and concessions of the early 1980s, the pattern of valuing job security less while demanding greater rewards or freedom from work stems directly from the nation's uninterrupted rise toward affluence.

It is not yet clear what impact the stagnant economy and declining real incomes beginning in the mid-1970s will have on worker attitudes. Workers have not become blind to harsh economic realities in spite of rising expectations, and the importance of job security in hard times is already apparent in union concessions in 1982 collective bargaining agreements. Yet these union "give-backs" may prove to be temporary and limited in scope, reflecting short term adjustments rather than long term shifts in worker attitudes. The permanence of changes in the outlook of workers accustomed to prosperity will depend largely on the severity of economic conditions which lie ahead.

Even if rising expectations are dampened by periods of economic hardship, the potential for restlessness and dissatisfaction among young workers seems particularly high. Concentrated in the lowest paid, lowest skilled jobs, younger workers are also the most educated in terms of years in school and exposure to news media ideas and information. The young are the least satisfied with the status quo, the least likely to be financially burdened, the least tempered by the knowledge of economic depression and the least impressed by value of job security. Unfamiliar with the nagging suspicion that all boom times must end, the younger worker has less inclination to buckle down or to provide for the future. While restrained by periodic recessions, today's younger worker still tends to assume that there will be a way to "get by no matter what."

The emergence of new work attitudes has been more visible in recent years because young workers represent an increasing percentage of the labor force. In 1960, only 16 percent of all workers were under age 24, compared with 24 percent two decades later. Of course, the proportion of youthful workers in the labor market will dwindle as the century draws to a close. In the meantime, however, younger workers will exert a major influence on work attitudes, exhibiting the rising expectations and growing impatience characteristic of the "new worker." Their actions and attitudes are wisely viewed as a barometer of broader changes working their way through society, changes which will eventually touch all segments of a rich and democratically educated society.

*"Don't worry! They'll grow up
to be great computer programmers!"*

In the 1970s, the portrait of the "new workers" often served as the focal point for discussions of the "decaying work ethic." A decade later, it seems far less likely that younger workers will become a force for reform at the workplace. The young may be the least patient with unrewarding work, but they remain concerned with their success in the labor market. If their affluence and extended education leave them with high expectations, the result more frequently is a heightened interest in "good careers" rather than a rejection of occupational goals. The most volatile segment of tomorrow's workforce surely will not be filled with the graduates of medical, business and law schools so popular among today's youth. It will be comprised of those groups who have not shared in the affluence which raises expectations, whose most basic hopes have remained unfulfilled.

Discrimination and Broken Promises

For the young, the implicit promises of the educational system heighten their sense of disappointment with labor market realities. For minority and female workers, the promises themselves have been more explicit—including assurances of equal opportunity and greater advancement to correct past patterns of employment discrimination. While government efforts to end discrimination have brought some gains in this area, the pace of progress has been relatively slow and almost surely unequal to the rise in expectations triggered by these initiatives. This disparity between promise and reality maintains race and sex, like age, as significant variables in job satisfaction trends.

The advances of blacks and women in the labor market over the past two decades are noteworthy (Table 6-2). The proportion of black professionals and managers has doubled in the last 20 years, while the relative number working as laborers or in service industries has dropped considerably. In 1960, more than two-and-a-half times as many blacks were blue-collar workers as white-collar, but now this ratio is nearly equal. The gains of women in the labor force are masked to some extent by their increasing participation in re-

Table 6-2   Females and Blacks Continue to be Employed in Low Paid Occupations

Occupation	Percent of total who are female		Percent of total who are black	
	1960	1981	1960	1981
Total Labor Force	**33**	**43**	**11**	**11**
White-collar	42	54	4	9
Professional and technical	36	45	4	9
Managers, officials and proprietors	16	27	3	5
Sales	40	45	2	5
Clerical	68	81	5	11
Blue-collar	15	19	12	13
Craftworkers and foremen	3	6	5	8
Operatives	28	32	12	15
Nonfarm laborers	2	12	27	16
Service workers	65	62	27	19
Private household	98	97	50	32
Farm workers	18	18	16	7

Sources: *Employment and Earnings Report*, January 1982, pp. 165-166; and *1981 Employment and Training Report of the President*, pp. 149 and 151.

cent years, but they have been significant. While the size of the female workforce jumped by 25 percent during the past two decades, the number of women managers increased by 44 percent. The percentage of female professionals has grown since 1960, while the proportion of women working in service industries has fallen.

The distribution of jobs in the economy remains skewed to the detriment of blacks and women, however, reflecting the legacy of traditional patterns of employment discrimination. Blacks, though comprising only 11 percent of the labor force, hold 15 percent of all operative, 18 percent of laborer, and 20 percent of service jobs. Even the shift from blue-collar toward white-collar work by blacks has been achieved primarily through growth in relatively low-paid sales and clerical fields. The traditional divisions of labor are equally apparent in the employment of women—they remain heavily concentrated in clerical and service roles, which constitute more than half of total female employment. While cultural biases keep women underrepresented in menial blue-collar jobs, they also have less than their share of managerial positions and break into professional roles primarily in the sex-typed occupations of nurse and schoolteacher. Some of the aggregate data on female employment may seem encouraging, but cashiers, waitresses, bookkeepers, secretaries and typists continue to dominate the ranks of working women.

In addition to a narrower and less attractive range of occupational choices, minorities and women are more likely to suffer from fluctuations and uncertainties in the labor market. Invariably, relatively more blacks than whites and more women than men are pushed onto the unemployment line during recessions, and even in periods of healthy economic growth, a disproportionate share of blacks and women are unable to find work. When employed, they receive an average wage well below that of their white, male counterparts. And not surprisingly, minorities and women are heavily represented among Americans living in poverty, either because they cannot obtain jobs or because their pay is too meager to support themselves and their families.

For studies of work satisfaction, these facts offer one basic lesson—in an era of presumed enlightenment and equal opportunity, even gradual improvements may lead to increased frustration and bitterness if accompanied by more rapid rises in expectations. Current data on expressed dissatisfaction reflect this gap between expectations and the labor market realities of groups suffering continuing employment discrimination, with blacks on the average almost twice as likely to be dissatisfied with their jobs as whites and women more than one-and-a-half times as likely to be displeased with their work roles as men. These relationships weaken when the analysis accounts for variables such as income, but the earnings potential of blacks and women are an integral part of the discrimination problem and not usefully separated in this manner.

It is unclear to what extent black and female workers found hope in government initiatives to combat discrimination at the workplace, or how much their rising expectations have outdistanced actual improvements in the labor market. Yet certainly minorities and women have been affected by recent gains in educational attainment and by the growing awareness of an "information society," leaving them more likely than ever before to be conscious of the disparities between their plight and the successes of others. The longer that equal employment opportunity remains a goal instead of a reality, the greater the chance that black and female workers will be disillusioned by seemingly broken promises.

The Impetus for Change

It is premature to argue that a radical transformation is underway at the modern workplace. The feared decay of the "work ethic" has not unleashed an exodus of workers from their jobs, and the data on worker satisfaction suggest a prevalence of mixed emotions regarding work more than widespread disaffection. Yet the cumulative impact of changes in the labor market on work satisfaction in the years ahead cannot be as easily dismissed. Even if the quality of work does not deteriorate, tomorrow's workers may expect and demand more from their job and be more impatient in awaiting results.

Current changes in the labor force are particularly important because they are unique to this era and not likely to be reversed. Despite lags in real income growth during the late 1970s, the most likely scenarios for America's future include ever richer, better educated and more sophisticated workers. This outcome is neither inexorable nor preordained, as ecological, political, economic or military catastrophes could overturn this progress. Yet should these trends of affluence and education continue, they may shape a workforce more volatile than known in any prior generation.

A steady rise in societal affluence will have a particularly adverse impact on labor force participants who do not receive a portion of its benefits. Already, poor prospects in the regular labor market have forced disadvantaged workers out of the mainstream of American society and into the underground economy.[7] Of course, much of this "black market" work arises out of efforts to avoid taxation, but a substantial portion must also be linked to the failure of the legal economy to generate sufficient jobs paying adequate wages. Such shifts toward the underground economy are consistent with dual labor market hypotheses, and are yet another indication of the possible polarization of American society in the absence of efforts to provide legal work for the least fortunate.

Current labor market trends, therefore, suggest that the impetus for change at the workplace will come from two very different directions. Persons employed in desirable jobs are likely to take past gains for granted and to seek improvements (in both wages and job content) to meet their rising expectations. In contrast, individuals in poor jobs or without work are likely to become increasingly disenchanted with the disparity between their fate and the advantages enjoyed by others, reacting either with resentment or withdrawal. The demands for change among the fortunate will be felt most strongly by employers themselves, while pressures for action from disadvantaged workers will be focused on public policy. In either case, the call will be for both work "reform" and for steps to meet the more basic goal of a job for all who desire one.

7 Work Reform in Perspective

> Distribute the earth as you
> will, the principal question
> remains inexorable—Who is
> to dig it? Which of us, in
> brief word, is to do the hard
> and dirty work for the rest . . . .
>
> —John Ruskin
> *Sesame and Lilies*

The concern for workers' satisfaction has culminated in attempts to reform work. Basing their proposals on concepts of alienation, analysts of the workplace have advocated a wide-ranging redesign of work roles and organizations. Rejecting the view that technology and efficiency mandate narrow and unsatisfying jobs, these reformers assert that rewarding work roles are not only consistent with efficient organization but actually stimulate higher productivity. Presumably, everyone gains under these enlightened approaches to the form and substance of work.

The dominant concerns of work reformers have changed over time. The debate of the 1960s and early 1970s focused primarily on narrower issues of job redesign and work organization, while more recent proposals have addressed broad themes of worker participation in "quality-of-

141

worklife'' programs and ''quality circles.'' Many work reform concepts have evolved over a much longer period, and the rediscovery of the quality of work is often akin to the proverbial old wine in new bottles. On a practical basis, unions and employers have been dealing with issues of work satisfaction for as long as they have been in existence, and the array of sociologists, psychologists and business consultants who now advocate work reform are relative latecomers to the scene. The modern critics of work may shift the emphasis of the work quality debate, but their claims are no more vital to workers than the traditional concerns of labor and management.

It is important to place work reform efforts in a historical perspective before judging the latest collection of proposals. Few methods of work organization have gone untried, and few suggestions for changes in the design of work are without precedent. Some very direct and meaningful improvements in the quality of work won through union activism are totally ignored by contemporary analysts, who sound as though gains in compensation, health and safety are somehow less significant than the more abstract goals of interesting and rewarding job tasks. Management initiatives in work reform parallel this long record of union activity, as employers in even the earliest stages of industrialization attempted to cope with an unruly and turbulent labor force. Both union and management attempts to raise the quality of work have brought successes, but they also illustrate the limitations of work reform which plague such efforts in a modern era.

Union Role in the Design of Work

Since the inception of the organized labor movement, work has been affected by the continuing efforts of workers to combat and compromise the power of their employers to determine working conditions and job content. The battle has been waged on many fronts—from the most basic terms of compensation to the establishment of work standards, the protection of worker health and safety, the introduction of new production technologies and the protection of individual rights. Years of bargaining have gradually given workers a voice in some aspects of work content and job design, and the evolved system of industrial jurisprudence has established a set of worker rights which limit the prerogatives of management to seek maximum output and efficiency. Though technological and market forces have largely dictated the tasks that must be performed, the collective pressure of organized workers has channeled, directed and at times even controlled the use of human labor in the modern workplace.

The historic role of unions in the design of work has been an important part of the work reform movement. Those who suggest that union leaders are out of touch with discontented memberships and have been slow to join the bandwagon for work reform are ignoring the traditional union accomplishments. The pay, leisure (including rest periods), fringe benefits and work standards on which union bargainers have concentrated are not peripheral to the "quality of work"; to a large extent they determine this quality. There is some reason to believe—as discussed in the next chapter—that unions may underemphasize less tangible aspects of work satisfaction in traditional collective bargaining efforts. Yet, on the whole, labor leaders have not been insensitive to the desires of their members—they simply recognize that unpleasant tasks will not disappear through work reform, and they seek the best possible combination of benefits and working conditions while accomplishing these tasks. The result has been some very significant advances in the lot of American workers, and the process continues.

Health and Safety

The most direct contribution of union bargaining to the quality of work has come in the area of occupational health and safety. Although managements have often been free to establish what work will be done, the line has generally been drawn at jobs which are particularly dangerous or unhealthy. In the early years of this century, organized labor was instrumental in outlawing the use of phosphorus and lead in manufacturing processes. Over the years collective bargaining has sought changes in job methods and procedures to limit dangers in high-risk occupations. The elaborate rules which govern mine safety and the various precautions required in construction and heavy manufacturing are the best examples of union-initiated improvements in industries where management had neglected the adoption of health and safety standards. Organized labor's goal of uniform standards was realized in large measure in 1970 with congressional approval of the Occupational Safety and Health Act, which covers all but the smallest workplaces and also provides for federal enforcement of these newly-won guarantees.

*"Back before the safety laws,
we had some **real** horror stories."*

In addition to this concern for overly dangerous or unhealthy working conditions, unions, particularly at the shop level, have been continually concerned with improving unpleasant or uncomfortable working conditions. Ventilation, lighting, cleanliness, bathroom facilities, cafeterias, parking, and innumerable other factors related to the workplace have been the object of union negotiations. Although such improvements cannot change the nature of jobs, collectively they may significantly raise the quality of work.

Pay and Work Standards

While the scope of labor-management negotiations has been broadened considerably over the years, the system of collective bargaining was originally conceived as a mechanism for obtaining a fair price for labor. The steady rise in real wages enjoyed by American workers provides the most concrete evidence of the effectiveness of union efforts, but pressures from organized labor have also had a direct influence on work standards. Whether the pay is by the piece or by the hour, the issues of compensation and production standards are frequently inseparable—normal work methods and speeds are an important variable in determining fair pay rates, and conversely, the pay rate dictates how much and how quickly work must be done. For this reason, unions in quest of higher wages continually attempt to keep work norms at the lowest possible level, challenging the employer's right to demand maximum effort for minimum wages. These struggles over standards of work unquestionably affect the quality of work, and work rules negotiated by unions continue to be a major source of labor-management conflict in manufacturing industries.

Again, the concern for work standards and quality is hardly new. In 1914, unions forestalled the adoption of Frederick Taylor's "scientific management" and succeeded in putting

"Taylorism" on the defensive by securing legislation which outlawed for a time the use of "a stop-watch or other time-measuring device, or a time study of any job" in federal facilities.[1] Four decades ago, production standards in the auto industry were not subject to the grievance procedures, but repeated strikes by workers who felt their interests were at stake have made this a subject of mutual negotiation. In 1946, a presidential conference aimed at avoiding strikes failed because management rejected the contention that unions should participate in the selection of production technologies, work standards and plant location. Yet in spite of a continuing ideological battle over appropriate labor roles, unions have had an undeniable impact on the design and quality of work.

Of course, the other way in which organized labor has bolstered compensation is through the regulation and reduction of work schedules. The most notable success has been the establishment of the 40-hour workweek, which has released workers from the endless cycle of dawn-to-dusk toil and fatigue. Additional leisure time has also been won through negotiated contracts guaranteeing vacation and sick leave rights, pensions that provide for earlier retirement, and more liberal lunch and break periods while on the job. Finally, unions have exacted premiums for overtime or shift differentials, thereby encouraging regular and convenient working hours. The cumulative effect of these changes in the quantity and scheduling of work has been jobs which are better paid, which offer greater freedom at the workplace and which require workers to spend fewer hours at the call of employers.

Technology

Organized labor has also fought to control the introduction of production technologies which not only threaten job security but frequently alter job content and the basis for determining fair compensation as well. Thus, as new and faster machines have come into use, unions have attempted to establish rules governing their operation and output. Though the number of workers rather than the quality of work is most often at issue, resistance to new technology certainly has affected the evolution of jobs, particularly in manufacturing sectors.

In many cases, unions have sought to prevent or delay the introduction of new methods or machines. Automatic glassmaking machines, stitchers and lasters in shoe manufacture, cigar rollers, paint sprayers, recorded music, automatic typesetters, and countless other innovations were vigorously resisted by unions because they decreased the skill or numbers of workers. In a few cases, the decline in the quality of work caused by new machinery was sufficient to lead unions to permanently limit the use of the new equipment. For example, the use of the hand granite surfacer, which was faster but more dangerous, was greatly restricted by the granite cutters' union.[2] Unions have rarely succeeded in preventing the use of a machine or process. More commonly, unions use wage and job security issues to limit the extent to which jobs are redesigned in response to new production technologies, thereby preserving some continuity in employment.

The mechanisms through which technological innovation and related production standards are controlled vary across industrial sectors. In the clothing industry, union-management councils establish the price per garment, effectively setting the work standards which must be maintained to afford decent wages. In other industries, management and unions negotiate the number of workers who must be employed to perform certain jobs without regard to need—the retention of firemen on diesel and electric trains many years after their work roles were rendered obsolete is a classic example. More commonly, companies offered no-layoff pledges to preempt union opposition to the introduction of computerized technology or similar innovations. Although these negotiations sometimes seek simply to preserve employment, more often they determine the quality of work as well. The number of workers on an assembly line makes a difference in work pressures, dictating the frequency of relief breaks, the intervals of repetition, and the speed with which operations must be performed.

When viewed collectively, the historic involvement of unions in shaping occupational safety and health, pay, work standards and technological innovation belies claims that organized labor has ignored issues of work quality. No doubt the reluctance of unions to embrace new and sweeping proposals has frustrated many contemporary work reform advocates, and there remains a fundamental conservatism in the attitudes of many union leaders. Yet the critiques of academics and management consultants may also prove less than objective; as one UAW representative observed, "It is easier to worry about boredom and forget noise, to write about monotony and ignore dust, to fret about dull jobs and not mention fumes on the job."[3] Even if the traditional goals of organized labor seem mundane and intellectually unstimulating, they remain meaningful and compelling on the shop floor.

Management and the Redesign of Work

The historical interest of organized workers in the quality of their work has been paralleled by similar concerns on the part of management. For employers, an apathetic or discontented workforce threatens productivity, no matter how efficient the technology or the work organization. The issue is less sociological or humanitarian than practical: How do you elicit maximum effort from workers when neither the job itself nor its monetary incentives inspire this commitment? Workers are approached as motivational problems, and improvements in work quality are contemplated as solutions. In contrast to the perspective of unions, enhanced satisfaction is seen primarily as a means rather than an end in itself.

Sophisticated management science in recent years has argued against such distinctions between union and management concerns, claiming that they both seek the efficient use of individual capabilities. According to modern theories of work reform, the most productive and profitable use of human labor necessarily implies structuring jobs which challenge and satisfy workers. In practice the distinction is not so easily erased, reflecting a tension between goals of work satisfaction and profit maximization which renders cooperative labor-management initiatives in work reform tentative at best. Particularly in the case of factory technology, efficient production and human fulfillment rarely ride along the same set of rails and, when they do, they may easily collide.

Regardless of its distinct emphasis, however, active management interest in aspects of work quality and satisfaction also has a history much longer than commonly understood. The earliest management efforts to raise productivity and profits through greater attention to the motivation of workers are now taken for granted—they include detailed studies of worker efficiency, improved amenities at the workplace, and institutionalized approaches to overall personnel management. These adaptations in management styles have provided the foundation for the much more elaborate concepts of work reform currently under consideration.

Specialization and Scientific Management

Throughout most of the industrial era, factories were designed with the goal of maximizing output per input units of labor and materials, but with little regard for the treatment of the individual worker. During this period, specialization and minute subdivision of tasks were adopted as the guiding principles in designing jobs, primarily because simplified jobs allowed the use of unskilled, low-paid workers. Moreover, specialization entailed less waste of time and materials in training and increased productivity because workers could become more proficient at their small tasks. Each worker could accomplish more because the wasted transition time between tasks and tools were eliminated. These efficiencies were, and remain, valid arguments for specialization; subdivided tasks continue to offer the potential for reducing production costs in many work settings.

The pattern of neglecting workers in the search for optimum efficiency in production systems persisted into the twentieth century. A pool of workers ready to accept harsh factory employment was always available, and more could be imported, as needed. Managers found little incentive to worry about motivating workers or improving the quality of work. In the crudest terms, most employers considered workers to be no more than cheap alternatives to machines. Only with a series of engineering innovations championed by Frederick Taylor and others did the role of the worker in the efficient design of work begin to receive serious attention.

Taylor, a worker turned engineer, had long analyzed impediments to efficiency resulting from the inherent conflicts between managers and workers. As one who had been on both sides of the fence, Taylor was convinced that owners and workers share a common interest in maximizing production. Calling his system "scientific management," Taylor analyzed the most efficient methods of performing tasks, using time and motion studies to determine the quickest way to accomplish the most work. Linking these redesigned work methods with incentive payments for increased output, he believed he could increase wages and improve the lot of workers while simultaneously increasing production and profits. By ensuring that workers performed their jobs with the utmost physical efficiency and were paid in ways which encouraged maximum effort, Taylor argued that the goals of both management and labor could be served.[4]

Taylor failed to recognize the uses to which his rigorous analysis of tasks would be put, and he overstated the consonance between individual and corporate goals. Rather than aiding workers, Taylor's engineering analysis became an extension of efficient work organization, in which specialized tasks were rigorously analyzed and further divided. Individual work roles became narrower, more controlled, and less satisfying than ever. Still, he was one of the first practical designers of work who was concerned with human variables in work. Although his name has since been associated by some with "inhuman" work arrangements, Taylor's own aims included the design of jobs which challenged and motivated workers and paid them higher wages.

Employee Welfare

Taylor's methods of scientific management were widely adopted during the first two decades of this century because they contributed directly to increased efficiency. So-called "welfare management," which came into vogue at about the same time, was less profitable. According to the Labor Department's description, welfare management was "anything for the comfort or improvement, intellectual or social, of the employees, over and above wages paid, which is not a necessity of the industry nor required by law."[5] These benefits might include subsidized or free cafeterias, libraries, athletic fields, beautified work surroundings, medical and dental care, safety programs, social organizations, company housing, or whatever other amenities might help to obtain the loyalty and support of employees.

Diverse factors contributed to the institution of these "welfare" programs. In some cases the humanitarian inclinations of the owners were being carried out; in others welfare work was a public relations gambit and, frequently, an effort to combat union organizing drives. Most often, however, the systems were founded on the hope that contented workers would be docile and more productive. Increasingly, companies viewed their workforces as investments to be protected and nurtured. During World War I, labor force turnover had risen to astounding proportions among factory workers, averaging above 8 percent per month.[6] Faced with labor discontent and militant unions, companies logically sought to co-opt workers by providing them with conspicuously improved working conditions and benefits.

Welfare management was never widely adopted. The decreasing number of immigrants (who had been the most receptive subjects for these blandishments) and the rise of organized labor limited the success of corporate attempts to obtain the allegiance of their workers. More importantly, a rise in unemployment in 1921 dropped turnover drastically and eliminated much of the reason for the "coddling" of workers. Many companies cut back sharply on their frills, and such broad corporate responsibility for employees' welfare was seldom reimplemented on this scale. The benefit packages of major corporations today bear a superficial resemblance to the "welfare" policies of sixty years ago, but the intent now is as much to attract workers as to co-opt them.

Personnel Management

The corporate awareness of the need to adopt more sophisticated and effective ways of dealing with workers did not vanish with welfare management. The worker had been discovered as a variable factor in the efficiency of an organization, one which employers attempted to influence and control through elaborate personnel policies. Separate personnel departments became the rule in large organizations, and employee relations emerged as a major concern in corporate management.

Throughout the next fifty years, personnel policies were steadily designed and refined in an attempt to ensure smooth organizational functioning and maximum productivity. Procedures for screening, testing, and training workers were combined with a variety of welfare benefits designed to stimulate company loyalty. Supervisory techniques and organizational relationships were analyzed to ease conflict and friction among workers and to promote efficient realization of corporate goals. Job evaluation techniques were pursued to give structures and pay differentials an aura of objectivity. All of these steps reflected a concerted effort to institutionalize responses to potential worker discontent and to include the worker in equations for efficient production systems.

These early peripheral adjustments in workplace amenities and management techniques seldom extended to the actual design of work tasks. While a variety of devices were used to mitigate problems of worker dissatisfaction and to suppress unrest, the primary motivator and satisfier of the workforce remained wage payments. Whatever the effect of work upon the worker, it was still assumed that a decent wage, tolerable working conditions, and a minimum of fringe benefits could buy a tractable workforce.

Modern Concepts of Work Design

Changes in the workforce and the structure of the modern corporation led to a reevaluation of traditional management styles. Following World War II, the growth of applied science in industry brought increasing numbers of scientists, engineers and other specialists into corporate environments. Similarly, the continuing expansion of corporate structures to produce, market and distribute huge quantities of goods increased the proportion of professionals, managers and other white-collar workers on corporate payrolls. When coupled with rising educational attainment in the labor force and the organization of workers in stable unions, many companies found themselves confronting a more ambitious and demanding workforce which resisted established personnel practices.

Today's employers have ample opportunity to respond to these shifts in the composition of their workforce. Attention devoted to worker motivation and improved personnel management may have always been justifiable, but it has become affordable only with the increasing affluence which now supports a plethora of administrators and consultants. Within recent years the swollen ranks of corporate management have emerged as a prime audience for the legion of industrial sociologists and psychologists who have joined the longstanding debate on the ideal organization of work. Rather than seeking simply to placate employees, "sophisticated" corporate executives are now assigned to pursue some of the finest nuances of work satisfaction and innovative management techniques.

Modern advocates of work reform have attempted to shift management attention from traditional adversarial postures, focusing instead on adapting work organizations to meet human needs. Their approach is decidedly optimistic, rejecting common notions that efficiency requires specialized jobs or that production technologies necessarily dictate work roles. As an alternative, modern concepts of work design claim that work environments and roles can be shaped to maximize worker satisfaction, and that the effort will actually enhance management goals of productivity and profit. Management and worker interests presumably can follow parallel paths.

The optimism of modern work reformers is also reflected in their views of human nature and work motivation.

Without stopping to offer evidence, most contemporary theorists portray the worker as an individual with great potential and, implicitly, with capabilities untapped by existing modes of work organization. Their concepts of individual needs and motivation arise largely out of the work of Maslow, Herzberg and McGregor, with an emphasis on the importance of appealing to higher-order needs for challenge and responsibility. Ultimately, the proposed models for improving work have been very similar, based on the following principles:

1. Jobs should allow the individual as much responsibility and autonomy as possible, including participation in decisionmaking with minimal authoritarian supervision.
2. Jobs should include tasks of meaningful size which provide each individual the opportunity to use broad and varied skills.
3. Workplaces should offer integrated social environments with room for personal interaction in healthy, pleasant surroundings.

The more obvious standards that workers value—good pay and substantial benefits—are sometimes implied but rarely dwelled upon.

As discussed earlier, it is not clear that all workers have the drive for fulfillment of higher-order needs which modern theories of work design project. The diversity of worker needs raises troubling issues for would-be work reformers, diminishing hopes of achieving job designs optimal for all individuals. Yet despite this limitation, the underlying assumptions of Maslow, Herzberg and McGregor have found their way into most modern critiques of work organization, applied not only to managerial and professional employees but to virtually all workers. Even if the more traditional rewards of pay and benefits are acknowledged to be important, critics of the workplace contend that it is the higher-order needs of workers which have suffered the most serious and costly neglect.

In the early 1970s, it was relatively easy to catalogue scores of significant experiments which advanced innovative forms of work redesign. The primary focus of these efforts, at least in theory, was the scope and structure of individual jobs. By the close of the 1970s, however, the emphasis had shifted from job restructuring to much broader attempts at worker participation, and management interest in work reform had grown dramatically. Literally hundreds of major U.S. corporations now have instituted some sort of work reform focusing on worker participation, real or illusory. The efforts are sold under different guises, but their major appeal to management lies in the hope that new work designs would help reverse recent declines in productivity and will also serve as an antidote to periodic labor unrest and discontent.

Enlarging and Enriching Jobs

The earlier ideas of modern work reformers stemmed from the belief that specialization had progressed beyond the point of maximum productive efficiency. Citing rising educational attainment and worker expectations in the labor force, the critics of the 1960s argued that narrow work roles failed to utilize worker skills and even discouraged work effort through monotony and close supervision. As an alternative to such confining methods of assigning or accomplishing work, reformers sought to instill a sense of personal achievement by expanding the number or kinds of tasks required in each job. This approach to work reform, often termed job "enlargement" or "enrichment," ultimately attempts to improve the match between job requirements and individual capabilities and thereby to enhance overall productivity among workers.

The most drastic of these innovations is the replacement of assembly-line manufacture with benchwork arrangements. Workers with small, highly fractionated jobs are given responsibility for a series of operations, or occasionally a full assembly and testing process. An example was a much-touted experiment by General Foods at its Gaines Pet Food plant in Topeka, Kansas. The company discarded the traditional asssembly-line methods and members of work teams performed as many different types of tasks as possible.[7] Similarly, both Motorola Corporation (Plantation, Florida) and Corning Glass (Bedford, Massachusetts) established factories in which individuals or small groups assembled, inspected, and tested entire electronic components or instruments.[8] While the permanence of results was suspect, the companies claimed at least short term successes, citing improved morale, lower absenteeism and turnover, and substantially better product quality. However, because the option of reorganizing work on any basis other than assembly-line manufacture usually is feasible only through new plant construction, such radical attempts to "enlarge" jobs have stimulated far more discussion than replication.

A less revolutionary approach to job enrichment is to allow workers to perform various jobs, relieving assembly-line monotony by giving each worker more tasks which must be repeated less often. One such attempt at job enlargement was tried at the Maytag Company—assembly and inspection of a new automatic washing machine was changed from a subdivided (average fifty-second interval) operation to a more complete job which took nine minutes to perform. Although training times were longer, the workers allegedly achieved levels of skill which put their productivity on a par with more fractionated methods.[9] Again, the Maytag program reportedly brought at least temporary improvements in worker attitudes and product quality.

Most critiques of the workplace have centered on blue-collar jobs and assembly-line production, but the concepts of job enlargement and rotation have been applied to white-collar work as well. In general, the goal has been to reassign tasks so that each worker has a share of both boring, undesirable duties and more pleasant, creative ones, ideally including supervision and inspection. AT&T initiated one of the earliest experiments in an office setting in 1965, assigning individuals complete modules of work in an attempt to cut turnover and improve productivity. Thus, telephone book assemblers were given the entire job of processing and verifying a section of a book, and billing clerks were given complete responsibility for certain accounts instead of a single operation on each account. Along with this job enlargement, numerous positions were "upgraded" and offices were redesigned to facilitate communication among employees with related jobs. The claimed results—presumably including reduced absenteeism and turnover, improved productivity and morale—attracted widespread attention in the work reform debate.[10]

A variety of companies have duplicated the AT&T methods. In most cases the emphasis has been on providing workers with a broader set of tasks and maximum freedom to accomplish them, a sharp contrast to the norm of fractionated work roles and strict supervision. Although workers have been little involved in the planning processes of these experiments, they are usually given a greater measure of control in the actual performance of their work. The potential for this expansion of job responsibilities is limited by skill and staffing levels, but apparently some companies have found room to reverse past trends toward highly telescoped work roles.

While interest in job design spawned numerous reform experiments, it should be noted that many such innovations were nothing more than improvements in the workplace. The renovation of workplaces to accommodate social interaction or work flow—whether through circular benchwork arrangements to facilitate conversation or the rearrangement of office furniture to facilitate interaction among members of work groups—hardly constitutes genuine work reform. Improved dining, lavatory, and parking facilities, the abolition of time clocks, and the substitution of salaries for hourly wages also aim at peripheral rather than structural features in job satisfaction. These approaches to poor worker morale may be effective, but they have less to do with the nature of work *per se* than with the amenities of the work environment and the differences in perceived status among various jobs. In this sense, such work "reforms" have familiar roots in the traditional union concern for worker dignity, supported now by management in the pursuit of improved morale and productivity.

Participative Management and Quality Circles

Partly in recognition of the technical and economic limits to job redesign, advocates of work reform in the 1970s shifted their focus to broader concepts of participative management, seeking to promote greater diffusion of responsibility and control in work organizations. The move toward participative management is intended to serve multiple goals: to more fully use the skills and information of workers; to enhance worker satisfaction; and to link to a greater extent the goals of the individual and the larger work organization. On the premise that even the most unpleasant jobs become more tolerable when workers have some voice in its overall planning and execution, work reformers have argued that worker participation provides a basis for identification with the firm's success. Experiments have run the gamut from suggestion boxes to autonomous work groups, but more time is needed to assess whether the fervor with which systems of participative management have been pursued will have a lasting effect.

As with most other work "innovations," the sharing of responsibility and control is not a new idea. The optimum delegation of authority and control to achieve given objectives has been debated at least since Jethro advised Moses on the organization of his chain of command, and has been thoroughly developed as a "science" in this century. Efforts to enlist workers' voluntary cooperation date as far back as profit sharing, an idea tried at the Bay State Shoe and Leather Company in 1867. Joint committees of management and labor have been tried at least since 1924 when the B&O Railroad instituted such a cooperative plan. The Elton Mayo pioneering studies in work teams at Western Electric Company and the profit sharing and worker suggestion systems developed by Joseph Scanlon are early examples of "participative management." Although current work designers are mostly concerned with the sharing of responsibility as it relates to individual autonomy and work satisfaction, their methods have ample precedent.

It is the systematic analysis and implementation of this principle of worker participation which is relatively new. Ranging from quality circles to "quality-of-worklife" programs, attempts at highly structured labor-management cooperation have proliferated in the last five years and now dominate the discussions of work reform advocates. For organized labor, any positive reactions to these new thrusts into participative management are based on prospects for improved job satisfaction; for example, a March 1979 conference of union officials examining quality-of-worklife improvement efforts defined the goal of such efforts as "the opportunity for employees at all levels in an organization to have substantial influence over their work environment by participating in decisions related to their work, thereby enhancing their self-esteem and satisfaction from their work."[11] Needless to say, management representatives come to quality-of-worklife programs with a somewhat different perspective, viewing participative management as a technique to improve worker morale and more importantly to increase productivity. In both cases, however, there remains a belief that meaningful participation can alter worker attitudes in a significant and constructive way.

The recent resurgence of interest in participative management is illustrated by the growing number of quality circles in American industries. Small committees in which management and labor representatives jointly analyze and solve production problems, these quality circles were first conceived by American consultants in the early 1950s, but were widely adopted only in Japan. As one factor in impressive quality control and productivity gains in Japanese industry, the concept attracted increasing attention in the mid-1970s and has now emerged as the latest fad in industrial management in the United States. Depending on what is counted and who is doing it, estimates of the number of American companies using quality circles range from 250 to 2,500, including such corporate giants as General Motors, American Airlines, and Honeywell Corporation.[12] Although a survey conducted for the International Association of Quality Circles indicated that many circles are "nothing more than monthly supervisors' meetings or traditional project committees set up to deal with problems identified by management," they certainly are an institutional mechanism through which worker participation efforts are channeled.[13]

The proliferation of quality circles, and the broader quality-of-worklife movement of which they are a part, are heralded by their advocates as offering diverse potential benefits for both management and labor. Irving Bluestone, the leading American union advocate of quality-of-worklife initiatives, has contended that such programs can lead to: more constructive collective bargaining; a more satisfied workforce; improved product quality and efficiency; and reductions in absenteeism, labor turnover, grievances and disciplinary actions.[14] Most of his fellow union leaders are less sanguine about the compatibility of management and worker interests, but increasingly there is a consensus that organized labor cannot ignore quality-of-worklife processes. And for management, quality circles and other participative management techniques are often viewed as the only alternative to deteriorating product quality and declining competitiveness in international markets. Notwithstanding expressions of humanitarian concern for worker satisfaction and fulfillment, firms rarely devote resources to quality-of-worklife programs without an expectation of tangible results in the form of enhanced profits.

Of course, the crucial distinction between various quality-of-worklife efforts is the extent to which they actually delegate responsibility and control to workers. Nearly all companies find it advantageous to encourage voluntary cooperation from their employees, and yet few are willing to give broad policymaking authority to workers. Between the extremes, the varieties of shared responsibility and control come in every shade of gray, making it difficult to gauge the significance and effectiveness of the overall quality-of-worklife movement. Meaningful diffusion of responsibility and control is important to the success of participative management models, for only a clear sense of influence will convince workers that their participation and ideas are taken seriously. The desire of managers to elicit worker participation and thus achieve greater productivity while preserving traditional decisionmaking prerogatives creates the fundamental tension in quality-of-worklife schemes, and it is on the establishment of an acceptable balance that the success or failure of such projects depends.

A few examples help illustrate the range of options utilized in delegating authority to workers. In one of the oldest and most widely noted experiments in participative management, Donnelly Mirrors Corporation of Holland, Michigan, transferred responsibility for virtually the entire production function of the business to the workers on the line. A small company supplying mirrors to the auto industry with a long history of profit sharing and open labor-management communication, Donnelly became a model of work reform nearly two decades ago by dividing employees into task-oriented teams responsible for setting and reaching production goals. The workers were given the authority to control the assembly pace and the assignment of jobs along the line. In addition, all employees received salaries rather than hourly wages, collectively setting the rates at which they would be paid but also holding the responsibility for implementing the productivity increases which must support pay raises. Under this system, the company enjoyed marked improvements in product quality and manufacturing efficiency, making its program one of the most successful of its kind.[15]

"The management seems concerned that we're spending too much time on this topic."

This ambitious participative management technique—in which fully autonomous work groups determine production quotas, work methods, job assignments, and pay rates independently of higher level management—has been tried only infrequently and has generated few long term success stories. The full-scale diffusion of responsibility and control was attempted at Weyerhauser Lumber Company in Tacoma, Washington and resulted in some significant cost savings, but over time a number of autonomous production units failed to reach management-set standards and were abandoned.[16] Similarly, an in-depth study of work groups initiated at Sound, Incorporated in Los Angeles concluded that the most innovative attempts to give workers decision-making authority failed to get off the ground.[17] It is not surprising that most companies still view the wholesale diffusion of production responsibilities as more of a risk than they are prepared to take.

The mainstream of contemporary quality-of-worklife programs is typified by a hybrid of traditional and innovative management styles, in which top management reserves unilateral rights to overrule quality circle or worker recommendations but must exercise such rights sparingly in order to preserve a spirit of meaningful participation. Thus, Westinghouse Electric Corporation has embraced a system of participative management based on a series of councils, committees and quality circles which deal with issues as diverse as the allocation of capital among production units and vandalism in worker restrooms.[18] General Motors and the United Auto Workers agreed in 1973 to form a national joint committee to improve the quality-of-worklife, and subsequently developed a set of guiding principles which have become the basis for at least fifty quality-of-worklife programs in local UAW-GM bargaining units, including a model program at the GM assembly plant in Tarrytown, New York.[19] The list of notable quality-of-worklife programs goes on and on—including Xerox, Polaroid, General Electric, Texas Instruments, Sperry Corporation, Digital Equipment and many smaller firms. While it is uncertain whether these innovations will pay off for either labor or management, it is at least clear that a significant number of companies, including major corporations, are willing to experiment with accepting workers as limited partners through participative management.

Work Reform in Europe

The debate surrounding the structure and implementation of work reform efforts has been more heated in Western Europe than in the United States. Virtually every major industrialized nation has its own record of work experiments addressing problems of worker satisfaction and productivity, including numerous attempts by manufacturers in England and on the Continent to develop more humanized jobs in factories. European trade unions have succeeded in establishing a much stronger pattern of industrial democracy than ever contemplated in the United States, with substantial control of production frequently delegated to worker councils or representatives. In general, the concept of worker participation is less foreign to the history and management psychology of European firms, and work innovations have been tied more closely to government policies and union demands.

Studies on autonomous work groups and worker motivation were pioneered by the Tavistock Institute of Human Relations, founded in England in 1946. The Institute's early research among coal and textile workers spawned a wide range of work reform initiatives throughout Europe in the 1950s and 1960s. In its continuing work on employee motivation and satisfaction, the Institute has examined issues of work reorganization, industrial democracy, and the impact of organizational and legal structures on the process of worker participation in Europe. Its landmark studies on worker attitudes have shaped much of the subsequent debate on work reform, and its contributions continue to move that discussion forward in the 1980s.

As in the United States, numerous work reform experiments in European nations have concentrated on relatively narrow issues of job redesign. Attempts at Saab and Volvo plants in Sweden to avoid the worst aspects of auto assembly-line work, through both job enlargement and the creation of work teams which assemble entire vehicles, gained widespread media attention. In France, considerable attention has been given to the architectural design of work environments and the size of production units as important factors in work satisfaction.[20] West Germany has supported experiments in work reorganization, and the government's program has been criticized for assisting companies in worker safety and automation initiatives more appropriately financed by the firms themselves.[21] In all of these cases, the study of job design has addressed concerns for occupational health and safety as well as less tangible areas of psychological stress and job satisfaction.

State programs in France and West Germany are significant because they have linked issues of work organization with broader strategies for economic modernization and with responses to larger socio-technological problems.[22] Believing that a movement away from short work cycles and conventional assembly-line techniques will enhance productivity and international competitiveness, the German government spent about $42 million on "humanization" projects, with its Ministry of Research and Technology reimbursing employers for 50 percent of the direct cost of restructuring a work operation and retraining workers. The French government played a similar role in promoting work reform—legislation passed in 1973 created the national agency for the improvement of working conditions, which publishes periodic reports on trends in work reform and also subsidizes experimental projects in private industry. The willingness of the German and French governments to devote public resources to work reform experiments is in stark contrast to the lack of United States' public involvement in such activities.

The concept of worker participation and control has also been developed in European countries to a far greater extent than in American firms. In Yugoslavia, production systems in which small teams determine production goals and job assignments while reaping the benefits of productivity gains have flourished since the end of World War II. Trade unions in Scandinavia have had sufficient muscle to secure government mandates guaranteeing worker participation in the decisions of private companies and sharply curtailing management prerogatives in a wide range of areas. A 1977 Swedish law required full disclosure of information related to management decisions and removed limitations on the sphere of collective bargaining so that even decisions on investment policy and plant location could be subject to union negotiations.[23] Similarly, a 1977 Norway law included far-reaching demands for the reduction of stress and monotony at the workplace, for variability and opportunities for personal development in jobs, and for self-determination in the labor process.[24] While union leaders in both countries have concentrated their efforts on occupational health and safety and less concrete participation and job content mandates have proven difficult to enforce, the policy changes themselves reflect the level of interest and commitment to work reform and enhanced worker participation.

The contrast between American and European models of industrial relations is most clearly illustrated by cultural perspectives on codetermination, the direct participation of labor representatives in company management. With higher levels of unionization and greater politicization of European unions, codetermination has become an integral part of worker participation mechanisms in West Germany, Sweden, and Norway, and has drawn increasing attention in France and Italy. Yet the codetermination model has been coolly received in the United States—by management and labor alike. Noted labor economist Jack Barbash has argued that codetermination "runs against the grain of the American way in industrial management," rejected by management for fear of losing control and by labor for fear of losing bargaining effectiveness through shared responsibility.[25] The president of the Communications Workers of America, Glenn E. Watts, put the union position succinctly when he remarked,"I don't want to sit on the board and be responsible for managing the business. I want to be free as a unionist to criticize management."[26]

This adversarial tenor of American industrial relations also plays an extremely important role in distinguishing between work reform experiments in the United States and Japanese models of participative management currently in vogue. While Japanese concepts of quality control and innovation may be applicable in some circumstances to American firms, the cultural differences which separate workers in Japan and the United States seriously limit the relevance of Japanese models of work organization to American problems. American labor exhibits neither the heightened class consciousness of its European counterparts nor the docility of Japanese workers. It occupies a middle ground characterized by a practical distrust of management, resisting both the internalization of corporate goals and the ideological pursuit of anticorporate sentiments through class-based political action. The structure of American industrial relations is not immutable—as but one example, it seems possible that conservative economic policies embraced in the early 1980s will lead to a period of greater political activism by unions. Yet the historical development of labor-management relations does define both the prospects of and limits to change at the American workplace.

The Importance of Reform Experiments

The attention focused on experiments to redesign jobs stemmed originally from the publicized notion of the "alienated" worker, but the impact of work reform has now stretched well beyond that narrow discussion of job satisfaction. Even if no crisis of discontent is in sight, the discovery that work in many cases can be reorganized while still meeting productivity and profit goals is of humanitarian interest. Menial and monotonous jobs requiring hard and dirty work are not new, but neither are they illusions created by work reformers—they simply are the continuing byproduct of an industrial system now populated by a less timid and less patient generation. On this basis alone, there is ample reason to believe that work reform experiments will continue and that new solutions to problems of undesirable work will be sought in an attempt to cope with rising expectations within the labor force.

The increasing awareness among management and labor of the potential for marginal improvements in work has been particularly encouraging. Although the basic concepts in modern work design experiments are familiar, the use of these techniques seems more common than even a decade ago. Similarly, while all workers may not strive for self-actualization through work, many will no doubt appreciate the benefits of more challenging and rewarding jobs. It is important to keep the rhetoric of work reformists in perspective, for the limits of job redesign and worker participation are at times severe. Yet by emphasizing the importance of workers as human capital, the advocates of work reform have made a lasting contribution to the quality of work for generations to come.

8 The Limits to Change

The fact is that the work which
improves the condition of mankind,
the work which extends knowledge
and increases power and enriches
literature, and elevates thought,
is not done to secure a living. It is
not the work of slaves, driven to
their task by the lash of a master
or by animal necessities. It is the
work of men who perform it for
their own sake, and not that they
may get more to eat or drink, or
wear, or display. In a state of
society where want is abolished,
work of this sort could be
enormously increased.

—Henry George,
Progress and Poverty

Reports of work reform experiments are almost always
"success" stories. These positive accounts are understand-
able—the literature is most often the product of reform advocates committed to change at the workplace. Yet a calmer
evaluation of the potential for work reform must recognize
the biases of such messianic tracts, and examine the full
range of experience in areas of job redesign and participative
management.

173

The tendency toward selective reporting of work reform results is impossible to ignore. Companies whose enrichment and participation plans turn sour rarely trumpet the news, just as consultants drawing fees for their advice have little incentive to emphasize the limits to work reform. Even journalists seeking good copy tend to overlook the continuing effectiveness of authoritarian controls and traditional job rewards while publicizing less representative innovations by employers. Although acclaimed experiments at the workplace do provide useful lessons as to what "works" and why, their achievements must be viewed in a realistic perspective which acknowledges the obstacles to long term and widespread change.

Permanence and Replicability

It is common for proponents of work reform to cite immediate gains in productivity, worker morale and product quality following the implementation of work innovations. Yet short term results of such efforts are not in themselves significant. As documented by industrial psychologists at Western Electric Company's Hawthorne plant in the 1920s, any change in management style, whether autocratic or democratic, may generate short term productivity gains—workers simply respond to expressions of management interest. This "Hawthorne effect" makes longitudinal studies of work reform experiments particularly important, and yet such long term analyses of work innovations remain extremely rare. In fairness to advocates of work reform, the difficulties of establishing rigorous controls and isolating other variables at the workplace are numerous, and management attempts at work reform usually emphasize tangible results rather than valid proofs of causal relationships. The inevitable record, however, is garbled accounts of productivity gains and tenuous assumptions about their origin, providing a weak research base for any claims of success.

If the productivity gains of work experiments are of indeterminate duration, changes in worker attitudes and morale may be even less permanent. Just as today's young union members may have little appreciation for the wages and working conditions won by earlier generations, so new workers in "humanized" plants may fail to find their work upgraded or more enjoyable. Those who are present for the change from assembly lines to benchwork, or those who remember the authoritarian supervision which preceded the introduction of participative management, may appreciate the better quality of their work. But positive reactions resulting from innovations inevitably fade as novel systems become routine, and new arrivals are likely to see only jobs with certain sets of tasks, wages, and bosses. An initial spurt of enthusiasm for redesigned work may objectively reflect "better" jobs, but there is ample reason to believe the long term result will be higher expectations rather than enhanced worker satisfaction.

The question of permanence is perhaps most critical in programs of participative management. Because an unwavering commitment to nontraditional management styles is essential to the continuing success of worker participation schemes, many initiatives falter when the novelty wears off. Managers may become frustrated with the demands of participative decisionmaking, and workers may become disillusioned with the slow pace of change or the limited extent of their influence. In either case, a sense of meaningful worker

participation is easier to create through work innovations
than it is to sustain over long periods of time. Unlike changes
in actual job design, the benefits of participative management are as ephemeral as the spirit of cooperation and open
communication from which they arise, and thus may
evaporate in the face of personnel changes and unfulfilled
expectations. Reports of the short term gains may encourage
reform advocates, but the true test of participative management efforts lies further down the road.

These transient and illusory characteristics of many work
reform attempts serve as important qualifications to the
literature describing such experiments. Yet even in those
cases in which lasting results are achieved through innovations at the workplace, the expansion or diffusion of successful reform methods has proven extremely difficult. In a
discussion of past work redesign initiatives, one observer
argued that successful case studies have left us with little
systematic knowledge of how to effectively organize work
activities, claiming that few experimental programs had been
replicated in other organizations or even diffused
throughout the organizations in which they were launched.[1]
Frequently, work reforms are undertaken in relatively small
companies on a comprehensive basis, or else become encap-
sulated in a particular unit of a larger corporation as a "pilot
project." In either event, new principles of work organization and design which can be clearly articulated and applied
in diverse work environments remain very limited.

There is considerable evidence to suggest that diffusion of
innovative work systems is inherently slow, particularly for
the more nebulous quality-of-worklife programs currently in
vogue. Initiatives in participative management tend to be
highly subjective and personalized, providing more a process
for improved communication than a standardized solution
for specific problems of work organization and design. For
this reason, even when quality-of-worklife programs offer

relative advantages over existing systems, they often are difficult to replicate—by nature they tend to conflict with established norms and values, to defy easy description, to pose risks of failure, and to threaten the authority and control of traditional decisionmakers.[2] Furthermore, for unit managers there is little to be gained by adopting a work design successfully tested in another branch of the organization. At best, credit for the diffusion is shared with the original designers, while responsibility for failure to replicate a "proven" model is likely to fall solely upon the unit manager.

The combined lack of permanence and replicability has led James O'Toole to conclude that almost all of the well-publicized efforts of the 1970s to restructure the work environment have failed to survive intact. Rather than thriving, he contends that "the general pattern—in more than 100 plants, ranging from a radio factory to a telephone company—is one of a brief leap forward followed by a prolonged backslide."[3] Although O'Toole attributes these failures to experimental designs which were monolithic, static, and insufficiently tied to monetary rewards, it seems that an exhaustive list of barriers to work reform would be considerably longer and that the very potential for improved work may be seriously limited.

Without question, some experiments in job redesign and participative management have produced promising results from the perspective of both management and labor. Reported gains in product quality, productivity and worker satisfaction cannot be totally dismissed, and yet they also may not represent the wave of the future for most organizations and workers. Such experiments focus heavily on manufacturing settings, a work environment which is increasingly dwarfed by the growth of the service sector. More importantly, even in this relatively narrow context, technological and economic forces seriously constrain alternative ways of organizing work. In the absence of fundamental revisions of our economic system, voluntary efforts at work reform will never transform the workplace, but will remain confined to narrow areas in which the common interests of labor and management are clear and compelling.

Technology and Job Redesign

The concept of redesigning or enriching jobs is fundamentally a challenge to the idea that technology dictates work organization and job definitions. To replace more traditional notions of technological determinism, work reform proponents suggest that there are a number of equally productive alternatives for job design within any technological framework, some of which exact greater human costs than others.

The goal of job enrichment is to correct what advocates view as a longstanding failure to consider the human costs of production alternatives—costs which some suggest will render modern organizations increasingly dysfunctional.[4] In this sense the plea for "enriched" or "humanized" jobs is coupled with a vision of vast, untapped human potential. A major advocate asserted:

> If only a small percentage of time and money that is now devoted to hygiene . . . were given to job enrichment efforts, the return in human satisfaction and economic gain would be one of the largest dividends that industry and society have ever reaped through their efforts at better personnel management.[5]

Not only can job redesign be accomplished with minimal effort, the argument goes, but it is an avenue for raising productivity through the more enlightened use of human resources.

The surge of interest in job design has not been without its useful contributions to accepted ways of dividing tasks at the workplace. At a basic level, the debate concerning job enrichment has counterbalanced overly narrow views of technological efficiency in which human resources are forgotten as important variables in the production process. For example, work reform advocates have succeeded in focusing discussion on the inefficiencies of excessive divisions of labor with extremely short and highly repetitive job cycles. It is very possible that some workers would be more productive if they had more interest in their work, and that job cycles of three or ten minutes would be less monotonous and more efficient than those of thirty seconds. Experiments in job redesign serve as reminders that workers themselves have some control over output and productive efficiency, and that at some point the pursuit of narrower goals of technological efficiency through greater specialization becomes counterproductive.

In their zeal, however, advocates of job redesign have often overstated their case, ignoring the constraints imposed by technology in the search for production efficiency. Even if technology is not an absolute determinant of job design, it remains a decisive influence in the great majority of work settings, particularly in manufacturing. Milling machines, computers, forklifts and arc welding techniques tend to dwarf any choices of task assignment in dictating the nature and scope of individual jobs. Particularly in mass production systems, there is little room for variation of work roles without decreasing productivity. The traditional structure of manufacturing industries has not evolved haphazardly—specialization may be costly in terms of human satisfaction, but it promises relatively cheap production. At some point, advocates of job enrichment clash directly with the logic which first spawned the division of labor as an essential ingredient of efficient mass production, overlooking the unprecedented advances which the assembly line has made possible.

A few attempts to depart radically from assembly-line production methods have met with some success, and yet the alternative systems of manufacture are applicable to only a small number of situations. For example, the widely heralded "benchwork" assembly methods at Motorola, Maytag, and Corning Glass involved products with small components, fairly lengthy assembly times, and few tools. Individual and small group assembly of whole items is much less feasible in industries which involve large units or complex, expensive tools—the inescapable logistics of storing and moving large components generally means that assembling cars or refrigerators or engines can be accomplished most efficiently on a conveyor belt. Even the reform-minded managers of Donnelly Mirrors realized that an assembly line, with specialized jobs and constantly paced synchronized operations, was essential to profitable mass production.

In industrial sectors where existing technologies are particularly rigid or oppressive, the benefits of work restructuring may be severely limited, offering "little more than a

Band-Aid.''[6] One critic of job enrichment efforts viewed the search for more "humanistic" designs as fundamentally at odds with production goals:

> Given . . . the basic nature of mass production, where can there possibly be opportunities for such highly individualistic activity as autonomy, creativity, and self-actualization? I am afraid there are few—if any at all.[7]

In many ways, the mass production of multiple, identical, consumer goods is dismally confining. The worker in an efficiently designed, machine-dominated factory is often a cog, performing jobs that cannot be deeply satisfying. While management techniques may have the potential for relieving pressures or enhancing self-esteem, the prospects for creating interesting or meaningful work roles in these settings are very slim.

Of course, the champions of job enrichment launch their arguments with appeals to the profit motive. They claim that the advantages of eliminating high turnover rates, raising product quality, decreasing waste, and tapping firsthand knowledge for design innovations justify improvements in work quality on economic grounds alone. Yet proponents of work reform ultimately seek to enlarge jobs, increase skills, lengthen job cycles or rotate tasks for the sake of workers themselves, as part of an effort to make work more "humane." In the extreme, this view becomes an argument for a return to craft production, characterized by more complex jobs with longer training times. When the true costs of job enrichment (including higher training costs, greater inventories, and duplication of tools) are tallied, such reforms are exposed as appealing but noncompetitive and thus of little interest to management. An automobile can be produced by craftsmen, but only at costs that few can afford.

Even when technological advance or creative engineering designs make possible more "humane" forms of work organization, the awesome capital investment necessary to revamp established methods of production poses a major barrier to job redesign. If manufacturing jobs have become hardened into molds cut generations ago, much of the reason lies in the physical plant and machinery accumulated over the years. Plants manufacturing durable goods contained an average of approximately $60,000 of fixed capital per worker in 1980, and these real costs are constantly rising. Particularly as automated machinery is introduced to ensure more stringent quality controls, the factory will become increasingly capital-intensive and even less susceptible to the dramatic reorganization of work processes. It is hardly surprising that the most innovative experiments in job redesign have been undertaken in newly-constructed facilities, without the limitations implicit in years of accumulated capital.

Changes at the workplace are painfully slow and evolutionary in nature. The design of jobs may be far from ideal in terms of potential job satisfaction, but they do reflect the plodding rate at which new technologies are adopted in a rational search for production efficiency. Industrial psychologists can sweep through factories unlocking executive toilets and removing time clocks, and such incidental improvements in the work environment may bolster worker morale. Yet the same workers and machines will be left to crank out coffee pots or card tables or cookie jars, with little flexibility to alter basic manufacturing processes. Placed in a realistic framework of technological change and production constraints in competitive markets, principles of job redesign can do little more than correct excessively narrow definitions of efficiency and remind us that workers remain a significant variable in the drive for improved productivity.

Common Interests and Participation

Just as the enthusiasm for job redesign has been based on an overly optimistic view of technology, the growing interest in participative management is rooted in a rose-colored vision of the commonality of interest between management and labor. Participative decisionmaking, profit sharing, and autonomous work arrangements all seek to unite the individual's goals with the firm's pursuit of profits. From an employer's perspective, the hope is that shared responsibility will cause workers to identify with the larger organization, and that an acceptance of the organization's aims will transform a monotonous job into a labor of love. Presumably, everyone wins under this enlightened management style—workers feel more important and thereby more satisfied, while management reaps the benefits of greater productivity and fewer disruptions at the workplace. Yet few proponents pause to examine the strength of this commonality of interest, and they ignore the tension between management and labor priorities which seriously limits the scope and significance of participative management efforts.

Except in the face of deep crisis, the goals of any sizable corporation and those of its employees are not easily harmonized. By its nature, the corporation is not primarily concerned with worker satisfaction, but rather is openly interested in profits and evaluates most other goals in relation to this single variable. Similarly, workers are concerned with improving their own lives, a goal only incidentally related to the corporation's success and often in direct conflict with the corporate drive for higher profits. Unless corporate enterprises radically alter their function to make the welfare of employees their first reason for being, the basis on which workers would fully embrace the firm's goals is hard to imagine. Management and labor simply have distinctly different sets of priorities and concerns at the workplace.

The tension between management and labor goals is revealed when the actual implementation of participative management is considered. For example, management respondents commenting on a recent labor conference on quality-of-worklife programs repeatedly voiced concerns that too much attention was being given to worker needs, noting that increased productivity and improved organizational effectiveness are among the key objectives which make management willing to spend time and money on participative management.[8] In a similar vein, while former UAW vice-president Irving Bluestone asserts that "democratizing the workplace and humanizing the job need not be matters of confrontation" between labor and management, he also expresses hope that the auto manufacturers will abandon "the historic trickle-down theory that profits come first, that profits exemplify good in themselves and can only redound to the benefit of society."[9] Amidst fears that the priorities of both parties will somehow be lost or forgotten, the common ground for labor-management cooperation seems much smaller than theorists suggest.

The distinction between labor and management interests is more than some abstract Marxist truism. Rather, the potential for conflict is apparent whenever the cost of work reforms becomes significant. Employers are acutely aware of what reform initiatives may cost, and they rarely pursue such innovations without the promise of long term payoffs in profit and productivity. More importantly, when work reform fails to produce benefits for management, the effort is quickly dropped even if it offers gains in worker satisfaction. The experience of one corporation, an early participant in job humanization experiments, illustrates the point: The owner was committed to improved work, but he abandoned the concept when profits plummeted, observing that "the purpose of business . . . is not to develop new theories of management."[10] A better lot for workers does not always translate into higher profits for employers, and few firms stick with experiments on humanitarian grounds alone.

Workers are no less disinterested in their approach to work reform. Few employees would give up a part of their compensation to support costs of job redesign or participative management, and many might reject "humanized" work if it meant accepting lower levels or even slower growth of wages. Furthermore, labor is wary of the source of higher profits and productivity stemming from work reform, believing that experiments at the workplace may simply elicit greater work effort without providing fair compensation in return by raising production standards, circumventing seniority systems, and upgrading skill levels while avoiding additional remuneration.[11] Particularly if they do not enjoy any of the benefits of reduced costs and higher productivity, workers may be justified in viewing work reform as part of a long tradition of management manipulation contrary to labor interests.

The adversarial relationship between labor and management is evident not only when considering the costs and benefits of work reform, but also when determining the extent of worker responsibility and control in participative management schemes. From a management perspective, the retention of control or ultimate decisionmaking authority is an integral part of profit maximization, and very few firms are so devoted to worker participation that they are willing to surrender "veto" powers over worker recommendations. Some employers may demonstrate a genuine interest in engaging workers in the solution of production problems, but beyond this narrow realm the goal is to give employees a "sense" of control without surrendering decisionmaking prerogatives. To the extent that meaningful influence and authority are withheld, such experiments in participative management may be rightly viewed by labor as shams, as sophisticated attempts at behavior modification. Yet the alternative—to relinquish actual control of production and profits to a group of workers—poses a threat to the very existence of the corporation in its traditional form.

In practical terms, the social and institutional forces resisting meaningful diffusion of responsibility and control are extremely powerful. As sociologist Robert Schrank has noted, the primary purpose of hierarchy is control, and any shift in the nature of control threatens those who might lose some authority.[12] Middle managers upon whom the success of more open, participative styles of management depend are only too frequently disposed toward autocratic forms of supervision and decisionmaking—this management approach fits nicely with traditional organizational structures, enriches managerial roles, and is consistent with the dominant behavior styles of both employees and managers in contemporary organizations. More innovative management styles not only require a distinctly different set of interpersonal skills, but they also run counter to the competitive instincts which are usually responsible for corporate survival and achievement. In this context, middle management has emerged as a major institutional barrier to even the most well-intentioned participative management efforts.

Supporters of worker participation are guilty not only of underestimating the divergence of labor and management goals—they can also be faulted for failing to acknowledge the strength of authoritarian and meritocratic norms embedded in American culture.[13] Throughout our society, we place great emphasis on individualism, on a competitive struggle for recognition and authority, so that the concept of collaborative decisionmaking and its implicit diffusion of responsibility and control is typically rejected in large American organizations as foreign and counterproductive. While most reform advocates discuss prospects for participative management as though these experiments were to be undertaken in a cultural vacuum, their effectiveness in reshaping the modern workplace is severely limited by strong philosophical and behavioral biases favoring authoritarian and hierarchical control. With managers and workers accustomed to other norms, the drive for acceptance of participative values will remain an uphill battle.

It is not surprising that American management has responded to these problems of diverging interests and cultural biases by establishing very modest objectives for worker participation. Rejecting the extremes of complete management manipulation or worker control, "quality circles" and related initiatives seek cooperation within relatively limited areas, hoping to establish some basis for improved communication between managers and workers while realizing marginal gains in productivity, product quality and profitability. Limited profit-sharing schemes sometimes are adopted as a means of strengthening worker commitment to such participative mechanisms, although even this distribution of profits can be only partial if management incentives to adopt work reforms are to be maintained. Workers typically are given a voice without gaining significant responsibility or authority, and therefore the likelihood that they "internalize" the firm's goals seems very slim. Employees who enjoy opportunities to voice their opinions and participate in joint undertakings may feel more satisfied with their jobs, but the adversarial tenor of American industrial relations will hardly be dispelled in the process.

The eventual success of participative management techniques depends largely on the relationship between managers and workers. Some advocates stress that positive attitude and commitment within managerial ranks are critical to the effectiveness of such work experiments, while other proponents have emphasized a presumably direct relationship between the scope of participation and improvements in morale, motivation and productivity. Unfortunately for work reformers, the intangibles of managerial behavior are extremely difficult to alter or influence in a systematic fashion, and the expansion of worker responsibility and decisionmaking authority heightens the risks of participative management, thereby diminishing its attractiveness. The useful lesson found in concepts of participative management is neither revolutionary nor complex, but perhaps far more useful in practice—any change in management style or decisionmaking which treats workers as individuals with ideas of potential value, rather than as cogs in a machine, is likely to allow workers a greater sense of dignity and foster a more positive attitude toward management and work as a whole. In this sense, even the simplest reforms to increase worker participation will have some humanistic value when adopted by enlightened and well-intentioned employers.

The Fallacies of Radical Work Reform

Inflated expectations for reforming work may often be traced in part to the redesigner's inaccurate or incomplete understanding of the job market and the workforce realities. Too frequently job redesign consultants seem to attack and "solve" problems which exist mostly in their imaginations.

Even when the problems of harsh or unsatisfying work do exist, reform speculations tend to ignore the basic technological and economic forces which created them and to offer solutions which are unworkable in a market context. Clearly there are some improvements in job design and worker participation which can be adopted in a manner consistent with societal norms and economic constraints, but to expect too much from the restructuring of jobs and work organizations is to invite disappointment and discontent.

In both job redesign and participative management, much of the work of reform advocates invokes a sense of nostalgia, wistfully seeking a return to an earlier era of industrial development. Jobs are to be enlarged toward the ideal of the highly skilled craftsman, and organizations are to be split into smaller units where the individual "doesn't get lost." Yet whatever the price that society is paying in terms of "dehumanized" jobs in monolithic, faceless organizations, it is unrealistic to hark back to a simpler world in which organizations were small and jobs were large, as though "paradise lost" could be regained. Specialized roles and specialized knowledge are essential to large organizations, and large organizations are unavoidable in an advanced society. Breaking up the corporation into small units with broad work roles may indeed be desirable from the standpoint of improving the quality of work, but it would not provide the efficient production which supports the tremendous affluence to which we have become accustomed.

Some critics of the modern workplace have gone so far as to reject the importance of economic efficiency as a necessary attribute of reformed work, arguing that the needs of workers should dictate the design and organization of production processes even if overall productivity is reduced. In this model of social efficiency, traditional economic costs presumably are to be balanced against the social costs of alienation, dissatisfaction, poor health and other products of unrewarding work. Yet any retreat from the productivity front to more primitive, costly, and "human" methods of manufacture would certainly occur only through governmental intervention, and most likely would not reflect the priorities and values of workers or of the majority of society. In a complex society seeking to support its growing population at an ever-rising standard of living and to pull in many more who were excluded from partaking in the rewards of an affluent society, the trends toward increased specialization and large hierarchical organizations are far more willful than accidental. The values and priorities conceivably could change, but at present we seem far away from placing work quality before affluence.

There is an inescapable irony in the debate over work reform and concepts of social efficiency. In a sense, the methods of production so decried for their low-quality work have spawned their own opposition, generating unprecedented standards of living which now provide the basis for criticisms of work quality. Without the tremendous affluence generated by efficient mass production, there would be no alternative lifestyles or occupations for workers to envy, and no time to invest in the education which has contributed to workers' dissatisfaction. Even while indulging in nostalgic longings for "better" work, there is little likelihood that the vast majority of current society would actually sacrifice more income in favor of a more "human" form of work. For now at least, it does not seem that we can afford both.

By ignoring the diversity of human interests and needs, work reform proponents run the risk of projecting their personal value systems on others as though there were a single, optimal approach to the design and organization of work. Advocates of job redesign have been the most specific in their criteria for "meaningful" work. For example, Louis Davis developed an exhaustive list of social objectives for job redesign, ranging from self-organization and self-control to independence, variety of job tasks, a sense of relationship to the larger production system and a basis for relating one's work to the outside community.[14] Yet, as one skeptic of such job redesign schemes put it, "It is not clear that all workers want job enrichment or that job enrichment alone, without increased wages, increased promotion opportunities, and a higher social status for blue-collar work, would resolve such blue-collar dissatisfaction as does exist."[15]

The desire for "challenging" work is far from universal. In initiating a team production system in its Westminster, Massachusetts plant, Digital Equipment Corporation found that only two of every three workers were interested in work requiring personal initiative as opposed to traditional assembly-line production.[16] Some workers who lack the aspiration for such changes and others who may favor authoritarian supervision find newly-redesigned jobs less than comforting. Reform advocates have oversold the need for change as well as their ability to effect it.

Experiments in participative management are less likely to impose values on workers (presumably participation is not mandatory), and yet these reform efforts highlight another sort of moral question. As already noted, the potential benefits reaped by management and labor under work reform programs are distinctly different—workers gain satisfaction while employers gain profits. Reform advocates hail this outcome as the basis for cooperation and common action at the workplace, but they ignore the very real sense in which workers can be manipulated and exploited under the guise of work reform. Because worker gains are so intangible, management is likely to be far more concerned that workers "feel" involved than than their participation is efficacious. One analyst wondered: "If management's gains are real, while workers' benefits are only in their minds, who has really benefitted?"[17]

Reform advocates have not only overlooked the diversity of worker interests and needs, they have also ignored the market mechanisms which foster evolutionary rather than cataclysmic change. To a considerable extent, the economic system provides a basis for determining whether a job is worth doing—employers decide what they are willing to pay, and workers what they are willing to accept. Assessments of overall job quality and satisfaction thus are reflected every year in myriads of individual decisions on what jobs to seek, which one to accept, at what level of compensation, and how long to remain on the job. While slack labor markets can severely limit worker choices, crises at the workplace are avoided largely because individuals change jobs and jobs themselves change. The market system cannot incorporate or address many goals, and it does not guarantee satisfying work, but its pricing mechanisms do respond in a way which promotes gradual shifts in both jobs and worker expectations.

Most prophecies of doom advanced by would-be work reformers ignore society's well-oiled machinery for matching workers to jobs. Should a particular task be deemed intolerable by workers, it will begin to price itself out of the market, increasingly left to machines or eliminated altogether. If job satisfaction ever assumes overwhelming importance among worker priorities, the existing structure of pay differentials and the mix of jobs itself will change considerably as these new priorities are at least crudely translated in the normal functioning of the labor market. Job satisfaction may take on a greater role in balancing the costs and benefits of employment, but it cannot alter the nature of the trade.

Of course, the range of choice confronting most workers is not unlimited, and particularly during times of high unemployment or within groups with limited skills the employment options may prove far less than desirable. The willingness to accept a job is not the same as liking it, and it is in this sense that job reformers are addressing real issues of growing importance. As greater education and affluence lift worker expectations to new levels, employers will have to respond in some way or face unrest in their workforce. Even now, innovations at the workplace offer the only hope for those trapped at the bottom of the labor market, whose problems alone warrant the attention devoted to work reform initiatives.

Reform innovations will gather greater force as they come to represent the wishes of workers, rather than those of productivity-minded managers or well-intentioned con-sultants. Many workers with demeaning jobs accurately perceive their work as unstimulating activity in the service of others, and they view collaborative efforts with their employers with deep skepticism. As bolt tighteners and machine watchers, they may seek to escape their work but carry few delusions about making those tasks somehow more challenging. When those workers become more prepared to demand changes in the nature and organization of their jobs, the work reform movement will have moved an important step beyond the manager's search for greater productivity and profits.

Union Response to Work Reform

Due to the importance of worker interest in attempts to restructure work, reform advocates have sharply criticized unions for their historical lack of enthusiasm for innovations at the workplace. Persuaded by the truth of their own message about the crying need for work reform, some of its ardent supporters have claimed that labor leaders who don't place work reform as a top priority on their agendas are out of touch with the rank and file and unaware of the scope of dissatisfaction at the workplace. Others have adopted a more reasoned approach, seeking to identify institutional barriers to union involvement in work reform. Yet virtually all observers concede that the response of organized labor will play an important role in the future of work reform efforts.

The most simplistic explanation of union disinterest in work reform—that union leaders do not know what their members want—is supported neither by evidence nor logic. The frequency with which members vote to reject settlements negotiated by their bargainers demonstrates that workers seldom keep their wishes secret, and the law guarantees them the right to express their wishes. Surely no outside urging was necessary to win workers' support for better pay, shorter hours, or improved working conditions. Similarly, the longest lasting models of participative management in the United States are the Scanlon plans, which were designed and instituted by union members. Given this record of union activism, the claim of stifled memberships seems less plausible than the alternative that union leaders and members just have not viewed work reform as crucially important.

Much of the detachment of organized labor from experiments in job redesign and participative management reflects a set of worker priorities which reform advocates prefer not to acknowledge. Before unions vigorously seek improvements in work, a majority of their members must feel such changes are worth striking for. At present, a majority of union members occasionally supports strikes over pay, leisure, pensions, job security and work rights, but they seldom protest the quality of their work in such walkouts. Furthermore, the leverage of organized labor on issues concerning the content and control of work is limited, as the self-interest of management has always far exceeded that of union members. While union negotiators may broach a few of these subjects as peripheral concerns, they will not be likely to stick by them under pressure until the rank and file is prepared to trade or risk other benefits for improvements in work quality.

There is some reason to believe that the structure and internal politics of labor organizations may cause union leaders to underemphasize less tangible quality-of-worklife issues in negotiations with management. Wages and other forms of compensation are easily quantified and universally desired by union members, while the value of gains in work quality is more subjective and may vary considerably for different segments of the membership. Pay increases can be spread across the entire workforce, while union efforts to eliminate or improve the worst jobs in a given factory or office would directly aid a few and do little or nothing to benefit other members. For this reason, work quality issues pose thorny political problems for union leaders, and it is hardly surprising that, in the absence of strident complaints from workers, they have maintained a more cautious approach by focusing on "bread and butter" issues of pay, benefits, work rules and occupational safety.

Nevertheless, the conservative and often skeptical reactions of unions to work reforms initiated by management is also fueled by past experience. Ever since the days of Frederick Taylor, management innovations at the workplace have been associated with work "speed ups" and other steps to raise employee output and effort without commensurate rewards. Workers are keenly aware of the profit motives which draw employers to these work reform ideas, and cannot avoid suspicions that management is pursuing subtle con games to manipulate labor. To them, absenteeism, turnover and disruptions on the job are not signs of a decaying work ethic, but simply the logical response to jobs that are not worth doing well, or perhaps not worth doing at all. Unions have little faith in the management and labor community of interest, and they display strong skepticism, if not hostility, to claims that work reform can transform lousy jobs into important or challenging work.

The most recent wave of interest in work reform has provoked concerns that quality circles and other forms of participative management pose direct threats to unionism, reflecting conscious efforts by employers to co-opt workers and to undermine traditional union goals. The bitterness of the political battle between management and labor during congressional consideration of labor law reform legislation in 1978 renewed fears of an all-out attack on organized labor, and the "humanization" of work is often viewed as part of this broader anti-union effort. No doubt many firms bring more benign motives to their reform programs, and a number of major unions have committed themselves to cooperative quality-of-worklife initiatives in spite of lingering skepticism. In some cases, organized labor actually may have little choice but to establish a role and a voice for itself in reform efforts, lest participative management schemes proceed without input from union representatives. Yet most work reform programs have started in nonunion shops, and the idea that they are designed partly to avoid future organizing efforts is anything but farfetched.

Amidst highly publicized union "give-backs" and concessions in 1982, some analysts have begun to speculate that harsh economic conditions as well as management initiatives may force unions to take cooperative efforts more seriously. There is no question that unions in declining industries, facing the worst recession in decades, have responded by exchanging wage concessions and labor prerogatives for greater job security. Yet outside of clearly troubled sectors—including automobile, rubber, steel and airline industries—the evidence in support of proclamations announcing a "new mood" of cooperation in American industrial relations is far from clear.[18]

For the future of work reform and participative management efforts, the issue is not whether labor has moderated its demands to reflect hard times, but rather whether it has altered its approach to collective bargaining and negotiation in fundamental and lasting ways. Former Labor Secretary John Dunlop contends that the current wage-concession trend is neither the sign of a new era of union-management relations nor especially important in the long run. Similarly, Daniel J. B. Mitchell of the University of California conducted a study of 45 cases of union concessions in 1981 and early 1982 and concluded that they did not represent "a sharp break from past behavior" or a significant change in historical patterns of negotiation.[19] In contrast, Jack Barbash and others view experiments with quality-of-worklife programs, codetermination, employee ownership and tripartitism as rudimentary forms of labor-management cooperation and as part of a larger trend fueled by poor economic conditions.[20]

The true test of such fledgling innovations will come during a period of economic prosperity, for only then will it be possible to distinguish between union responses to adversity and more permanent changes in labor attitudes toward management and contract negotiations. The basic adversarial structure of labor-management relations will no doubt remain in place following the current wave of "give-backs" and concessions, for the common interests of labor and management will continue to be limited. However, it is significant that labor leaders such as Victor Gotbaum are beginning to urge unions to pay greater attention to management's business, not as an exercise in altruism but rather out of a need "to recognize management's motives and options and to present alternatives."[21] Even if unions do not wish to accept the responsibilities of being managers, they may find it in their interest to understand the concerns of the opposition.

In the meantime, most unions will tend to view warily management initiatives to restructure work for fear that such efforts will become a means of co-opting their members. Limited gains in work quality will continue, as management and labor identify narrow issues of common concern or as unions slowly expand their traditional demands for improved working conditions. Yet knowing that the potential for "enriched" jobs or meaningful participation within management profit constraints is limited, unions are likely to place little stock in the voluntary overtures of management for improvements in the quality-of-worklife.

Means for Lasting Success

Work reform will remain inconsequential to most workers until they are willing to pursue improvements in work quality as rights secured through collective bargaining. When worker interest is spontaneous and vocal, job enrichment will develop as a logical extension of organized labor's demands on behalf of its members. Assuming that workers come to care enough about challenging and rewarding jobs to be willing to bargain and strike for them, unions will seek a voice in determining the content of jobs, further encroaching on management prerogatives. Bargaining may force the elimination or improvement of jobs which workers find undesirable, and pay scales may reflect to a greater extent the intrinsic benefits of individual work roles. Such improvements in work quality under these conditions would not be subject to the whims of management or the profitability of such innovations, but would be secured as benefits by organized labor in the same lasting manner that more traditional forms of compensation are now won.

When sufficient interest is aroused, the mechanisms for union pursuit of improved work quality will be familiar ones. The kinds of demands which unions might make through collective bargaining and to which employers might acquiesce include:

1. *Special rewards to those with undesirable jobs:* Workers with harsh or unchallenging jobs might receive extra holidays, more flexible work hours, or higher wages, providing incentives for management to improve or eliminate these work roles.

2. *A voice in the design of new production systems:* Unions might seek an opportunity to evaluate or comment upon new methods of production, or they might even push for a system through which they could pressure management to abandon undesirable changes.

A threat of strikes or abandonment of jobs would have
far greater impact when work plans were still on the
drawing board than when such innovations had already
been introduced on the factory floor.

3. *Expand occupational safety and health legislation:*
Following European models, organized labor might
work to expand coverage under existing occupational
safety and health laws so as to encompass harmful
physical and psychological effects of monotonous or
unchallenging jobs. Some further research might be
necessary to defend such an effort, but surely the health
of workers can be interpreted to include more than their
protection from imminent physical danger.

4. *Participation in overall management decisions:* Short of
codetermination, unions might insist on a greater role in
the setting of production goals or the allocation of investment capital as decisions which influence the quality
of worklife. The scope of such demands will depend
partly on future interpretations of the proper adversarial role and focus for organized labor.

The willingness of workers to pursue these further steps
toward controlling their worklives is not clear, for such gains
only will be secured in at least partial exchange for a slower
rate of growth in traditional union benefits. Yet if productivity resumes its historical growth and as the affluence of
American workers continues to increase, they may become
more and more willing to trade marginal amounts of pay and
benefits for more challenging work environments. If that
shift in attitudes occurs, advocates will neither have to plead
for the adoption of work reforms nor justify their value in
terms of management profits.

9 The Future of Work

You ask . . . why I go on working.
I go on working for the same reason
a hen goes on laying eggs.

—H.L. Mencken
Letter to Will Durant

Most predictions about the future of work are speculations based on straight-line forecasts of a single trend or even
an isolated event. A rise in unemployment is cited to support
the prognosis that society will soon have little use for the
labor of most citizens. Rapid advances in computers arouse
forebodings that workers will soon be "future shocked" by
the baffling complexity of their jobs or replaced by bat-
talions of robots. Incidents of worker unrest supposedly
threaten impending crises and demand radical work reforms.
More optimistically, successful efforts to redesign certain
jobs or to elicit worker participation are hailed as precursors
of an era in which all jobs will be "humanized." Each theme
traces a single thread, but fails to examine the broader social
fabric of which it is a part.

Even while illuminating important facets of work, these
monolithic forecasts offer misleading half-truths about its
future. Current trends are extrapolated to an extreme, with
little or no thought given to factors which would limit the
scope or slow the pace of such change. While would-be
reformers and self-proclaimed seers find visions of a

dramatically new future appealing, a gradual evolution of the workforce and of work itself is far more likely in a complex and diverse society. Not ignoring the disturbing developments in the labor market, there are also major causes for optimism usually overlooked by work's prophets of doom.

Familiar Prophecies

None of the dubious notions advanced about the future of work have been more persistent than the idea that work will someday disappear. Whether the result of an alleged waning of commitment among workers or of a compelling wave of technological advance, such prophecies portray a workless society in which civilization withers from lack of productive challenge. While one could imagine a "leisure society" characterized by unprecedented diversity and cultural development, most choose to conjure visions of a population dead-ending itself in front of a television set or perpetually lost in drug-induced euphoria. Implicit in these warnings is the assumption that leisure time would not be spent wisely by the great majority of the populace, an argument reminiscent of the debate over the 40-hour week which occurred a century ago.

When the actual patterns of work and leisure are more closely examined, images of a workless society are quickly dispelled. No reasonable reading of current trends, including gains in leisure time, supports the conclusion that jobs will become anachronisms even in the distant future. Despite phenomenal productivity gains, the labor force remains a steady or slightly rising percentage of the population, and women are virtually stampeding into the labor market. Concurrently, demands for goods and services have unflaggingly kept abreast or ahead of the economy's production and show no signs of giving up the race. Concern over the disintegration of the "work ethic" is more an uncritical and literal acceptance of presumed dedication to work in eras past that existed in the writings of moralists. In fact, today's workers continue to toil for reasons very similar to those of their predecessors. Even if they expect more at the workplace, most Americans still find reasons to remain employed.

Contrary to the gloomy forecasts of some futurists, the opportunity to work has also not lagged far behind the desire to work. While robots and other computerized technologies will make inroads in the production of goods and the delivery of services, there is good reason to believe that the expanding tasks which society deems necessary will maintain aggregate employment levels. As manual work has been mechanized, it has been replaced with mental effort; if minds are to be computerized into obsolescence, then work may be redefined to include emotional or spiritual labor. Already the work of psychiatrists, social workers, clergymen and related professions involves less manual or rational effort than emotional support, and in an affluent society the demand for such "human" services can be expected to rise even faster than the decline in more traditional production roles. The new technologies of the workplace will have some far-reaching consequences for our lives, but widespread joblessness is not likely to be among them.

Service Work

The trend toward greater leisure for American workers is clear and significant, but those predicting the demise of work have misjudged the nature of this shift. Aside from earlier retirement, the expansion of leisure time in recent years has not come through an exodus of workers from the market-place, but rather through the gradual growth of holidays, vacation, and other forms of paid leisure as well as through increases in the number of part-time workers. For individuals, the gains in leisure time have come in small increments and as part of a changing mix of work and leisure, rendering the visions of a workless society largely irrelevant. And because the demand for greater leisure arises from a workforce of ever-increasing affluence and education, even the assumption that Americans would be unable to cope with their new-found leisure seems highly questionable.

Although less dramatic than predictions of the disappearance of work for most members of society, recent claims of widespread worker dissatisfaction enjoy no stronger support from current labor market trends. While some workers are undoubtedly frustrated or unhappy in their jobs, it seems certain that this reaction has always characterized a portion of the workforce engaged in unpleasant and unrewarding tasks. Contemporary studies of work satisfaction are plagued by methodological uncertainties, offering no guidance as to how worker attitudes have changed over time and frequently reflecting the biases of survey questions more than the concerns of labor force participants. The problems of undesirable jobs certainly should not be ignored, for they continue to exact a significant toll from workers in the form of poor health, personal suffering and lost potential. Yet the evidence does not suggest that the feelings of this generation of workers are unique, and prophecies of widespread revolt at the workplace have gone unfulfilled.

The concern for worker satisfaction has spawned some useful experiments with the design and organization of work, and their lessons may help to alleviate some of the strains at the workplace in years ahead. As is often the case, the most zealous advocates of work reform have pressed their point too far, losing sight of the technological and economic forces which limit the feasibility of job redesign and participative management schemes in practical work settings. Given the dichotomy of labor and management interests, the day in which all work will be "humanized" appears far off, and pragmatic attempts to implement work innovations in the meantime will be necessarily restricted to rather narrow areas of cooperative activity. These realities of the labor market offer a more reliable basis for sketching a vision of the workplace of the future than visions of futurists who predict a social order where workers will perform only "meaningful" and attractive labor.

Sources of Optimism

In some ways, the general tone of most visions of the future of work is surprising. Regardless of whether one believes any specific scenario of impending change, the emphasis on potential crises in the literature leaves an impression that the next few decades at the workplace at best will be typified by the successful aversion of various pitfalls and catastrophes. Perhaps it is the inclination of consultants to search for problems in need of resolution, or perhaps just the habit of most people to take evolutionary improvements for granted. Yet for whatever reason, causes for considerable optimism which are clearly apparent in current labor market trends have been overlooked in most accounts of the future of work.

The most basic sources of promise and hope are the strong and unwavering trends toward greater affluence and leisure in American society, fueled by dramatic gains in productivity during this century. In 1900 a workforce of 29 million labored approximately 80 billion hours to produce a gross national product of $154 billion (in 1980 dollars). In 1980 an average of 97 million people worked 182 billion hours to advance it to $2,626 billion. An hour of labor which produced the equivalent of less than $2.00 in goods and services in 1900 produced $14.00 in 1980. While lagging productivity growth in recent years has prompted some concern regarding the permanence and future magnitude of this overall trend, the most likely scenario is that national productivity will resume its upward climb.

Past gains in productivity have enabled the average American to enjoy both markedly higher incomes and additional leisure time. The extent of these gains has already been portrayed, and indeed they have occurred slowly enough to permit their full scope and significance to escape notice. Yet the affluence and leisure which rising productivity has made possible are now reshaping the nature of work in American society, and driving three distinct and hopeful trends: (1) the expansion of individual choice in work; (2) the removal of unpleasant or undesirable work; and (3) the growth of concern for human potential at the workplace. In this context, while increasing productivity may never pardon us from our term in the "workhouse," it seems certain to lighten the sentence.

Toward Choice in Work

Freedom of choice in employment is by any measure a luxury. In agrarian and early industrial eras, virtually all members of a family had to contribute to its support, and the range of work options for even the most fortunate was limited to a very few trades. Even today, the great majority of the labor force is confined by established rules which guarantee certain wages and demand certain hours, and comparatively few individuals are free to change jobs at will or to avoid employment entirely. But with the rise of multiple family earners and increasing wealth, the stranglehold of work is gradually relaxing. Once productivity resumes its historical trend, higher incomes will grant broad discretion in work to an unprecedented number of individuals, transfer payments will allow many to escape from jobs entirely, and accumulated wealth will make labor optional to hundreds of thousands more. In all cases, the degree of personal choice and control at work can be expected to expand steadily.

Commonplace signs of the movement toward choice in work abound. As wages have risen, absenteeism and intermittent or part-time job holding have become more feasible. Households are often able to support several nonworkers with the earnings of a single member, and those with two or more workers effectively reduce the risks of voluntary job changes. Children are now supported for many years during their education, and most wives have the option not to work even when freed from the burden of household chores. The development of extensive public and private retirement systems enables older workers to leave the labor force even when still able to work. All of these shifts have moved us slowly but steadily in the direction of greater choice in work for a larger portion of the labor force.

The option of not working currently is meaningful only at extreme ends of the economic spectrum. At the top end of the income scale, work has always been voluntary, whereas public and private transfer payments have provided an alternative to the most low-paying employment for society's poorest members. It is particularly significant that transfer incomes have grown dramatically in recent years, climbing in 1980 dollars from $8.2 billion in 1929 (prior to the New Deal) to $90 billion in 1963 (prior to the Great Society) and then to $318 billion by the time President Reagan took office. During this half century, transfer payments rose as a share of total disposable income from 1.8 percent to 17.5 percent. Should this trend continue as our society becomes more prosperous, increasing numbers of Americans will enjoy either a cushion of high income to mitigate the risks of job choices or a gradually rising "floor" under employment which offers an alternative to the most undesirable and low-paying work.

For the great majority of workers between these extremes, greater flexibility to choose desired work is a more realistic goal than any complete departure from the workplace. Rising levels of affluence and leisure have had a direct role in expanding this aspect of occupational choice as well. With higher incomes, households have a greater opportunity to develop their own financial cushions to protect against hard times and to weather short periods of unemployment during voluntary job transitions. Increased leisure has made it easier for workers to explore other career options while still retaining their present jobs. Finally, the prosperity of American society has triggered other developments which are closely linked to leisure and choice in work—most notably, rising levels of educational attainment and improvements in home and transportation technologies.

Mass education has not only raised expectations but expanded the range of occupational choices for most individuals. Even a high school education postpones occupational decisions and provides limited chances to explore alternative job opportunities before entering any particular field. Pursuit of a college education offers even greater opportunities to test and alter career choices or to tailor educational programs for specific jobs—for example, the would-be doctor who has no stomach for dissecting frogs or the aspiring astronomer who has no facility for numbers will discover these shortcomings in time to switch occupational futures without great difficulty. These opportunities do not guarantee that graduates and their professions will be perfectly matched, but the chances that individuals will be satisfied with their eventual work roles are certainly improved.

Choice in work has also been promoted by advances in home and transportation technologies. A few decades ago most individuals were confined to the endless routines of homemaking, or confined to employment within a narrow circumference of their homes. Today's workers accomplish most of their daily maintenance tasks with little time and effort and are free to travel substantial distances to take jobs of their choosing. Despite the criticism leveled at unreliable gadgetry and wasteful automobiles, these machines have certainly released people to pursue the activities which they prefer. The future undoubtedly promises greater freedom along these lines.

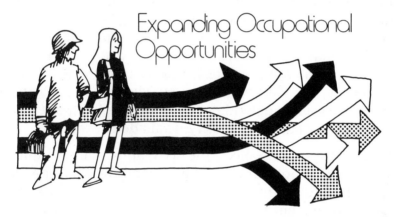

Expanding Occupational Opportunities

Clearly, a plethora of factors have contributed to expanded control and choice of employment. Lengthening prework education, shrinking time spent on jobs, enlarged geographic mobility, the elimination of many routine daily tasks, the growth of various transfer payments, and the general diffusion of affluence have combined to make a person's job more an expression of his own decisions and less a function of his economic or social background. It is important to note that not all segments of the labor force enjoy this greater freedom of choice, and many Americans remain trapped in poor jobs or with few work options. Yet most individuals are increasingly free to choose their work rather than condemn-

ed to accept it, and they are able to make decisions based less
on what is most available than on what is most desirable.
Rising productivity and wealth will continue to weaken the
bonds which tie workers unwillingly to their jobs.

Eliminating Undesirable Work

Increasing choice will bring new pressures to bear on the
design and organization of work and is likely to hasten the
elimination of unpleasant or unrewarding jobs. To the extent
that workers are willing and able to demand more desirable
work, their interests will become a significant force for
change at tomorrow's workplace. The worst jobs will be
shunned by growing majorities, forcing some employers
either to raise wages or to eliminate the jobs. Where
organizational changes and job redesign can upgrade work,
there will be intense pressure for these improvements. Most
importantly, the work which society chooses to accomplish
will be increasingly determined by what workers want to do,
as well as by what tasks society wants done.

Under any circumstances, the occupational mix within the
labor market is not static. As the demand for goods and services shifts and production technologies change, many of the
worst jobs are automated or in some way improved (including by better pay). While work reform advocates
repeatedly use examples of assembly lines, steel and textile
mills, and machine tool factories to bolster their arguments,
workers in these settings represent a small and dwindling
portion of the labor force. The job problems in some of
these fields remain serious, but the workers in these industries constitute only a tiny fraction of the expanding
workforce and considerable incentives to phase out the least
desirable work roles already exist. The rising expectations
and expanding job choices of workers will simply accelerate
this natural progression of technological advance in a
modern era.

The prospect of eliminating harsh employment is one of the most positive results of recent advances in robotics and other computerized technologies. Although the impact of automation on individual workers may be severe, the long-range effect on occupational structure will be to remove workers from the most dangerous and debilitating work roles. The monotony of assembly lines will be gradually borne by robots which do not mind the tedium, and the hazards of welding, material handling and sundry other jobs will be experienced by costly machines which can be damaged but not hurt. The process of eliminating undesirable work will be necessarily slow and not without its own human and economic costs, but it will represent one of the most significant trends shaping the future of work in the coming decades.

The rise in worker expectations and expansion of occupational choice will ensure that the quality of work becomes an increasingly important issue at the workplace. In a very rich and educated society, it is possible that money and leisure rewards may become less important social issues than the redistribution of creative and responsible work. As workers' freedom grows, pressure to restructure jobs may lead to the acceptance of reforms which are deemed unrealistic today. Such "enlightened" revisions by employers will not emerge from any newly-discovered sense of humanism or philanthropy, but rather from very direct economic pressures to maintain a stable and competent set of workers amidst an increasingly selective labor force. In those cases where new technologies do not improve the quality of work in large-scale production, manufacturing employers will progressively be forced to find their new employees in pools of surplus labor filled with the poor and undereducated. Advancing technology alone will not upgrade all jobs, and yet the monetary and leisure incentives required to man industries with rigid and undesirable work roles may escalate sharply as the economy develops alternate jobs.

So long as significant sectors of society remain unemployed and underemployed, no sellers' market for industrial labor will develop. Still, the growing awareness in society that each person should have a right to choose work will undoubtedly place factory employers at a disadvantage. The greater the value society places on meaningful work, the more rewards workers at monotonous and unchallenging jobs will be able to demand for their labor. Workers in those roles will pursue an already familiar path—they will radically divide their lives, putting up with hours of drudgery at work while seeking more money and more time off in which to enjoy this expanding supply of goods and services. Some will make the trade more willingly than others, but as a group they will steadily decline in numbers as technological change and worker priorities whittle away the most unpleasant and unrewarding work.

Workers as Human Resources

The same forces which are accelerating the elimination of undesirable work are also drawing increasing attention to the productive potential of workers themselves. Most discussions focus on the negative side of the issue, examining "problems" of worker dissatisfaction with unrewarding jobs, but the rediscovery of workers as a significant variable in production equations has an important positive side as well. In the face of growing pressures to respond to worker needs, both management and labor have begun to search for more effective ways to utilize individual capabilities and to reach previously untapped potential. It is a trend which promises both greater dignity for workers and more challenging or human work settings.

Again, signs of a fundamental change in attitudes toward workers are already apparent. Even if current experiments in participative management are not successful in promoting sustained collaboration between management and labor, they do indicate that the basic assumptions of traditional management styles are being seriously questioned—not only in academic classrooms, but also in corporate board rooms. Alternative styles of management designed to promote worker participation and tap worker knowledge are receiving increasing attention by progressive employers, and graduate programs in business administration at scores of institutions have been revised to include the study and practical application of such theories.

This heightened awareness of workers as valuable resources will not have the sweeping impact that reform advocates might hope. While the shift toward a collaborative style of decisionmaking in hierarchical work organizations can only bode well for the satisfaction of those who hang on to the bottom rungs, it remains to be seen how quickly these new attitudes will filter down to first-line managers who deal directly with and may be threatened by workers. Still, the renewed attention given to workers will give them some greater sense of dignity, and may correct poor job designs based on overly narrow concepts of technological efficiency. Yet once the tasks desired by society are determined, they cannot be greatly altered—chambermaids will continue to make beds, janitors sweep floors, gas station attendants pump gas, and garbage collectors, even if they are called sanitation engineers, still collect garbage. What we can hope for is marginal gains which will make some jobs more tolerable and which will alter the way in which future jobs are conceived and decisions made in modern work organizations.

Perhaps the most important outgrowth of a greater emphasis on workers as human resources will be the development of new government initiatives to create and channel discretionary employment. As previously discussed, a large portion of work in an affluent society is "non-essential," and the public sector plays a major role in allocating resources in pursuit of societal goals. Dramatic changes in manpower distribution are usually initiated only in the midst of serious national crises, but even routine government decisions channel workers into fields as diverse as space exploration, health care and public education. If the current surge of interest in human potential at the workplace extends far enough to affect popular values, government may devote increasing attention to the needs and desires of workers as well as to substantive goals of public policy in allocating discretionary resources and employment. Already, the debate over federal employment programs has come to emphasize the creation of "good" jobs as opposed to the subsidization of "make-work" employment. An affluent and sophisticated society may increasingly define the purpose of work not only by what is to be accomplished, but also by the human benefits of accomplishing it.

Clouds on the Horizon

There remain many reasons for being optimistic about the future of work in affluent, post-industrial societies. There are also a few sources of serious concern. The opportunities for exercising choice of work are steadily expanding, but such freedom is denied to a significant segment of the labor force. While undesirable work will gradually disappear, the process will be too slow to aid some workers and will preclude others from using the only occupational skills they possess. While most Americans will enjoy the fruits of rising productivity and societal wealth, a minority will be left behind in what may become a permanent underclass in an otherwise affluent society. In all cases, the prospect of a growing gap between the most and least fortunate challenges our basic concepts of equity and our quest for continuing social progress.

The rosy vision of a future in which individuals have ever-greater measures of choice in determining their work roles certainly is an empty mirage to those who have not shared in the economy's bounty. Choice in work is a luxury afforded to those with the incomes and leisure to pursue their own goals. For those who have been denied a share of the money and free time which prosperity has wrought, choice of work will be one more unattainable hope. Included in this group are the millions who are unemployed, the millions who are trapped in low-paying jobs, and the millions who cannot accept the risks of abandoning work they hate. Regardless of how bright the eventual prospects or how positive the current trends, society cannot ignore its responsibilities to these members at the bottom of the labor market.

As the gains in freedom of choice in work leave part of the workforce behind, so the advances brought by technological change have also failed to improve the lot of many workers. Because the processes of investment and automation occur relatively slowly, some Americans will continue to hold menial jobs for decades to come. The most dangerous work is likely to be automated or eliminated first, but the society in which all workers have challenging or rewarding roles remains far beyond our reach. Even the growth of the service sector, which appears to offer long term relief from the harsh work associated with assembly lines in manufacturing, will generate an ample share of unexciting and undesirable jobs for tomorrow's worker. Given the direction of changes in occupational mix fostered by technological advance, there is cause for encouragement, but the transformation of work advocated by would-be reformers will be a long time in coming.

The most disturbing threat to the welfare of workers posed by technological change is the displacement of those with narrow or limited skills. These problems are already becoming acute in declining manufacturing industries where unions have succeeded in achieving for their members relatively high pay—for example, in the domestic steel and auto industries. Individual skill levels offer little or no assurance of job security, and some of the most highly-skilled trades which typify well-paid blue-collar work will be rendered obsolete in an age of computerized design and production. Hardest hit by these occupational shifts will be middle-aged workers who have worked their entire lives in jobs requiring limited skills and offering little job mobility. Since areas of new employment growth will require skills much different from those needed in declining manufacturing sectors, the spectre of long term, structural unemployment for displaced workers must be taken seriously.

This problem of worker displacement, if unchecked by private and public remedies, will have a growing impact on both regional and national economies. Disparities in regional growth are already triggering stern warnings of a potential polarization of the nation's political system by region, with the Northeast and Midwest struggling to maintain levels of economic growth and political power now threatened by the burgeoning Sunbelt states. The concentration of displaced workers in areas of broader economic decline will make effective state and local responses to their employment ills considerably more difficult, and could heighten an already visible trend toward pockets of high unemployment and labor shortages existing side by side in different regions and sectors of the economy. Notwithstanding the tragic human suffering implicit in such a scenario, the costs of this pattern of occupational and geographic displacement in terms of lost productive capacity alone suggest the need to pursue an alternate course.

Finally, the long term future of work is clouded by the continuing exclusion of impoverished women, minorities and other jobless Americans from the harvest of growing prosperity. Even as choice in work and personal incomes increase for the majority of the labor force, disadvantaged subgroups continue to lag far behind either because of deficient education, lack of skills or discriminatory employment policies. Extremely high rates of joblessness among teenagers and minority groups serve as reminders that portions of the workforce are being left behind in a generally improving labor market, and that it may become increasingly difficult for these groups to catch up with or even to keep from falling further behind the affluent majority. It is this prospect of a permanent underclass, enjoying neither the hopes nor the benefits of future improvements in work, which must be averted by a just society.

Unfortunately, for the disadvantaged minority it appears as though things will get worse before they get better. After a long period of declining poverty levels (in both relative and absolute terms) responding to Great Society programs, the trend has reversed and the incidence of poverty in America is now rising. In 1978, 24.5 million people, or 11.4 percent of the population, were living in poverty. Only three years later, the ranks of the poor had swelled to 31.8 million, 14.0 percent of all Americans and rising. Economic growth alone will not correct this disturbing imbalance, and a narrow reliance on private sector initiatives can only generate a society in which the majority enjoys greater freedom and affluence while the rest languish in pockets of poverty, unemployment and broad economic decline. Given the significant cuts in income transfers initiated by the Reagan administration during its first year, such an expansion of the ranks of the poor now seems unavoidable.

Public Policy and Work's Future

For some, work is already becoming what they would "rather do anyway." For others—the hewers of wood and the drawers of water—no reform may ever make their work satisfying or worthwhile in its own right. The government has a responsibility to encourage a more equitable distribution of preferred jobs, and it can do so by arbitrating, within free labor markets, the rights of workers and the needs of society. Yet society should place top priority on ensuring that all who want jobs have them, that even the wages of the lowest-paid workers will support a decent standard of living, and that those who suffer temporary misfortunes are shielded from the market's harshest blows.

Public policy already plays a central role in cushioning the impact of economic uncertainties on labor force participants. Income transfers have placed a floor beneath many of those out of work, and job training programs have attempted to smooth the transition into new occupations. Public financing of education has also fostered greater choice in work, and thereby enhanced the control which individuals exercise over their worklives. In the absence of such direct and indirect government efforts to ease job changes and to reduce the suffering caused by economic cycles, the uncertainties of a market system would be far less acceptable to an affluent, democratic society.

The clouds on the horizon suggest that the role of public policy in shaping the future of work will be no less important in the years ahead. The problems of displaced workers and regional decline stemming from technological advances will be well beyond the reach of voluntary individual or collective action, and can be ameliorated through government intervention. Similarly, the disturbing abandonment in the early 1980s of governmental efforts to provide opportunities for work and training in the marketplace may fuel the growth of an American underclass populated with the unskilled and deficiently educated. The health of the larger economy and the rise of affluence and choice in work will offer no consolation to these groups who are increasingly left behind in the process of technological and economic change. It remains a public challenge and responsibility to include the least advantaged in the prosperity which our system has wrought.

Those who proclaim the demise of work have missed the mark. Work is surely here to stay, and it is only by virtue of the tremendous fruits of our labor that we can now contemplate more leisure time and greater choices in our selection of jobs. As we continue to rely upon work as the mainstay of our lives and our economy, we must also continue to search for the vehicles by which we can offer this role and its many benefits to all of society's members. Should we not fulfill this prime responsibility, the failings of work will be our own.

NOTES

Chapter 1

1. Sigmund Freud, *Civilization and its Discontents,* translated by James Strachey (New York: Norton, 1961), p. 46.

2. David Riesman, *Abundance for What?* (Garden City, NY: Doubleday, 1964), p. 151.

3. Daniel Bell, "The Cultural Contradictions of Capitalism," *The Public Interest,* Fall 1970, p. 38.

4. Christopher Lasch, *The Culture of Narcissism* (New York: Warner Books, 1979), p. 574.

5. John P. Robinson, "Toward a Post-Industrious Society," *Public Opinion,* August/September 1979, p. 46.

6. "Opinion Roundup," *Public Opinion,* August/September 1981, pp. 24-26.

7. George Katona and Burkhard Strumpel, *A New Economic Era* (New York: Elsevier North-Holland, 1978), p. 71.

8. Adam Smith, *The Wealth of Nations* (New York: Random House, 1937), pp. 4-5.

Chapter 2

1. Sebastian de Grazia, *Of Time, Work, and Leisure* (Garden City, NY: Anchor Books, 1964), pp. 1-56; Adriano Tilgher, *Homo Faber: Work Through the Ages* (Chicago: Regnery, 1965); and Wilbert Ellis Moore, *Man, Time, and Society* (New York: John Wiley, 1963).

2. Gerhard E. Lenski, *The Religious Factor* (Garden City, NY: Doubleday, 1961), pp. 4-5.

3. Robert Schrank, "Are Unions an Anachronism?" *Harvard Business Review,* September-October 1979, pp. 108-109.

4. Bernard Lefkowitz, *Break Time: Living Without Work in a Nine to Five World* (New York: Hawthorn Books, 1979), p. 98.

221

5. Rosabeth Moss Kanter, "Work in a New America," *Daedalus,* Winter 1978, p. 52.

6. Studs Terkel, *Working* (New York: Pantheon, 1971), p. 44.

7. John Coleman, *Blue-Collar Journal* (Philadelphia: Lippincott, 1974), p. 96.

8. The Bureau of National Affairs, Inc., *Current Developments,* July 24, 1980, p. A-7.

9. Harry Maurer, *Not Working* (New York: Holt, Rinehart and Winston, 1979), p. 1.

10. Lillian B. Rubin, *Women of a Certain Age: The Midlife Search for Self* (New York: Harper and Row, 1979), p. 59.

11. U.S. Department of Health, Education and Welfare, *Work in America* (Washington: U.S. Government Printing Office, 1972), pp. 8-9.

12. Betty Friedan, *The Feminine Mystique* (New York: Norton, 1963), p. 24.

13. John A. Garraty, *Unemployment in History* (New York: Harper and Row, 1978), p. 5.

14. Sigmund Freud, *Civilization and its Discontents,* translated by James Strachey (New York: Norton, 1961), p. 27.

15. U.S. Congress, House Committee on Education and Labor, *Hearings on Hours of Work* (Washington: U.S. Government Printing Office, 1963), p. 220.

Chapter 3

1. Juanita Kreps, ed., *Women and the American Economy: A Look to the 1980s* (Englewood Cliffs, NJ: Prentice-Hall, 1976), pp. 9, 63.

2. The Roper Organization, *The 1980 Virginia Slims American Women's Opinion Poll,* p. 35.

3. Arden Hall and Terry R. Johnson, "The Determinants of Planned Retirement Age," *Industrial and Labor Relations Review,* January 1980, p. 251.

4. Philip L. Rones, "Older Men—The Choice Between Work and Retirement," *Monthly Labor Review,* November 1978, p. 4.

5. Elliot Liebow, *Tally's Corner* (Boston: Little, Brown, 1967), p. 63.

6. Lester C. Thurow, *The Zero-Sum Society* (New York: Basic Books, 1980), pp. 64, 72-73.

7. Robert A. Moffitt, "The Negative Income Tax: Would it Discourage Work?" *Monthly Labor Review,* April 1981, pp. 23-27.

8. Janice Neipert Hedges and Daniel E. Taylor, "Recent Trends in Worktime," *Monthly Labor Review,* March 1980, p. 9.

9. U.S. Bureau of Labor Statistics, *Handbook of Labor Statistics* (Washington: U.S. Government Printing Office, 1980), Tables 52 and 86.

10. Hedges and Taylor, "Recent Trends in Worktime," p. 4.

Chapter 4

1. Harold L. Sheppard and Neal Q. Herrick, *Where Have All the Robots Gone?* (New York: The Free Press, 1972), p. xi.

2. Harvey Swados, Foreword to Sheppard and Herrick, *Where Have All the Robots Gone?* p. x.

3. Richard M. Nixon, Presidential Labor Day Address, September 6, 1971.

4. Karl Marx, *Early Writings,* edited and translated by T. B. Bottomore (New York: McGraw-Hill, 1963), p. 125.

5. Richard Schacht, *Alienation* (Garden City, NY: Doubleday, 1971), pp. 168-173.

6. Robert Blauner, *Alienation and Freedom* (Chicago: University of Chicago Press, 1964), p. 15.

7. Jacques Ellul, *The Technological Society* (New York: Alfred A. Knopf, 1964), p. 320.

8. Alvin Toffler, *The Third Wave* (New York: Bantam Books, 1980), pp. 17, 206.

9. Blauner, *Alienation and Freedom,* pp. 166-167.

10. Frederick I. Herzberg et al., *Motivation to Work* (New York: John Wiley, 1959).

11. Douglas McGregor, *The Human Side of Enterprise* (New York: McGraw-Hill, 1960).

12. Daniel Yankelovich, *New Rules* (New York: Random House, 1981), p. 44.

13. Ellul, *The Technological Society,* pp. 399-400.

14. Jerome M. Rosow, "Quality-of-Work-Life Issues for the 1980s," in *Work in America: The Decade Ahead,* Clark Kerr and Jerome M. Rosow, eds. (New York: Van Nostrand Reinhold, 1979), pp. 157-187.

15. Irving Bluestone, "Worker Participation in Decision Making," in *Humanizing the Workplace,* Roy P. Fairfield, ed. (Buffalo, NY: Prometheus Books, 1974), p. 54.

16. Lloyd Ulman, Robert Flanagan, and George Strauss, *Worker Discontent: Where Is the Problem?* (Berkeley: Institute of Industrial Relations, University of California, 1974).

17. Daniel E. Taylor, "Absent Workers and Lost Work Hours, May 1978," *Monthly Labor Review,* August 1979, p. 49.

18. U.S. Bureau of Labor Statistics, *Handbook of Labor Statistics* (Washington: U.S. Government Printing Office, 1980), Tables 167 and 170.

19. Robert P. Quinn and Graham L. Staines, *The 1977 Quality of Employment Survey* (Ann Arbor, MI: Institute for Social Research, The University of Michigan, 1979), pp. 212-213, 220.

20. Nancy Morse and Robert Weiss, "The Function and Meaning of Work," *American Sociological Review,* April 1966, pp. 191-198.

21. Yankelovich, *New Rules,* p. 152.

22. George Strauss, "Is There a Blue-Collar Revolt Against Work," in *Humanizing the Workplace,* p. 25.

23. *Ibid.,* p. 38. See also Jack Barbash, *Job Satisfaction Attitudes Surveys* (Paris: Organisation for Economic Co-operation and Development, 1976), p. 22.

24. Michael Crozier, *The World of the Office Worker* (Chicago: University of Chicago Press, 1971).

25. David McClelland, *The Achieving Society* (Princeton, NJ: Van Nostrand, 1961); Arthur N. Turner and Paul Lawrence, *Industrial Jobs and the Worker* (Cambridge: Harvard University Graduate School of

Business Administration, 1965); Charles Hulin and Milton R. Blood, "Job Enrichment, Industrial Differences, and Workers' Responses," *Psychological Bulletin* (1968), pp. 41-55; William F. Whyte, *Organizational Behavior* (Homewood, IL: Richard D. Irwin, 1969), chapter 32; and Wain W. Susjanen, et al., *Perspectives on Job Enrichment and Productivity* (Atlanta: Georgia State University, 1975).

26. Mitchell Fein, "The Myth of Job Enrichment," in *Humanizing the Workplace,* p. 73.

27. Quinn and Staines, *The 1977 Quality of Employment Survey,* pp. 48, 57.

28. William M. Winpisinger, "Job Satisfaction: A Union Response," *The American Federationist,* February 1971, p. 9.

29. Goran Palm, *The Flight From Work,* translated by Patrick Smith (Cambridge: Cambridge University Press, 1977), p. 16.

30. Blauner, *Alienation and Freedom,* pp. 29, 183.

31. Ellul, *The Technological Society,* p. 396.

Chapter 5

1. Organisation for Economic Co-operation and Development, *A Medium Term Strategy for Employment and Manpower Policies* (Paris: OECD, 1978).

2. Stanley Aronowitz, *False Promises* (New York: McGraw-Hill, 1973), p. 292.

3. Russell W. Rumberger, "The Changing Skill Requirements of Jobs in the United States," *Industrial and Labor Relations Review,* July 1981, pp. 578-590.

4. Colin Norman, *The God That Limps: Science and Technology in the Eighties* (New York: Norton, 1981), p. 113.

5. *Working Women,* "Race Against Time: Automation of the Office" (Cleveland: April 1980).

6. "Robots Join the Labor Force," *Business Week,* June 9, 1980, p. 62; and Joann S. Lublin, "As Robot Age Arrives . . . ," *Wall Street Journal,* October 26, 1981, p. 1.

7. Otto Friedrich, "The Robot Revolution," *Time,* December 8, 1980, p. 75.

8. Gene Bylinsky, "A New Industrial Revolution is on the Way," *Fortune,* October 5, 1981, pp. 106-114; and Barnaby J. Feder, "The Automated Research Lab," *The New York Times,* October 27, 1981, p. D1.

9. Herman Kahn, William Brown and Leon Martel, *The Next 200 Years* (New York: Morrow, 1976), pp. 8, 20-24.

10. Lublin, "As Robot Age Arrives . . . ," p. 1; and "The Speedup in Automation," *Business Week,* August 3, 1981, p. 62.

11. Senator Lloyd Bentsen, *Congressional Record* (daily edition), December 10, 1981, p. S14908.

12. Harley Shaiken, "Detroit Downsizes U.S. Jobs," *The Nation,* October 11, 1980.

13. Fred Reed, "The Robots Are Coming, The Robots Are Coming," *Next,* May/June 1980, p. 32.

14. "The Speedup in Automation," p. 62.

15. Diane Werneke, "Women and Microelectronics: The Impact of the Chip on Office Jobs," report prepared for the International Labour Office, December 1981, pp. 115-124.

16. Clive Jenkins and Barrie Sherman, *The Collapse of Work* (London: Eyre Methuen, 1979), p. 182.

17. Mick McLean, "Sector Report: The Electronics Industry," background study prepared for Organisation for Economic Cooperation and Development in *Technical Change and Economic Policy* (Paris: OECD, 1980).

18. Richard W. Riche, "Impact of New Electronic Technology," *Monthly Labor Review,* March 1982, p. 39.

19. Quoted in Reed, "The Robots Are Coming, The Robots Are Coming," pp. 37-38.

20. Lublin, "As Robot Age Arrives . . . ," p. 21.

21. William W. Winpisinger, "Correcting the Shortage of Skilled Workers," *The American Federationist,* June 1980, p. 21.

22. Theodore J. Gordon and Olaf Helmer, "Report on a Long-Range Forecasting Study," in *Social Technology* (New York: Basic Books, 1966), pp. 81-82.

23. James S. Albus, *People's Capitalism: The Economics of the Robot Revolution* (College Park, MD: New World Books, 1976); and Colin Hines and Graham Searle, *Automatic Unemployment* (London: Earth Resources Research Ltd., 1979).

24. Hesh Wiener, "The Robots Are Here, But Are They Helping?" *Business and Society Review,* Fall 1980, p. 37.

Chapter 6

1. Anne McDougall Young, "Trends in Educational Attainment Among Workers in the 1970s," *Monthly Labor Review,* July 1980, p. 46.

2. Ivar Berg, *Education and Jobs: The Great Training Robbery* (New York: Praeger, 1970).

3. University of Michigan, Survey Research Center, *Survey of Working Conditions, November 1970* (Washington: U.S. Government Printing Office, 1971), p. 406.

4. James O'Toole, "Education Is Education, and Work Is Work—Shall Ever the Twain Meet?" *Teachers College Record,* Fall 1979, p. 9.

5. Russell W. Rumberger, *Overeducation in the U.S. Labor Market* (New York: Praeger, 1981), p. 97.

6. William W. Winpisinger, "Correcting the Shortage of Skilled Workers," *The American Federationist,* June 1980, p. 22.

7. "The Underground Economy's Hidden Force," *Business Week,* April 5, 1982, p. 66.

Chapter 7

1. Don D. Lescohier, *Working Conditions,* in John R. Commons and Associates, *History of Labor in the United States, 1896-1932* (New York: Macmillan, 1935), Vol. 3, p. 314.

2. Sumner H. Slichter, *Union Policies and Industrial Management* (Washington: The Brookings Institution, 1941), p. 208.

3. Franklin Wallick, "Work with Dignity," in *Humanizing the Workplace*, Roy P. Fairfield, ed. (Buffalo, NY: PrometheusBooks, 1974), p. 67.

4. Frederick W. Taylor, *Shop Management* (New York: Harper, 1912).

5. Lescohier, *Working Conditions*, p. 316.

6. *Ibid.*, p. 331.

7. Richard E. Walton, "How to Counter Alienation in the Plant," *Harvard Business Review*, November-December 1972, pp. 70-81.

8. Claude Davis, "Manufacturing of the Pageboy II" (Schaumburg, IL: Motorola Communications, 1972), unpublished paper.

9. James F. Biggane and Paul A. Stewart, "Job Enlargement: A Case Study," in Louis E. Davis and James C. Taylor, eds., *Design of Jobs* (Middlesex, England: Penguin Books, 1972), pp. 264-277.

10. Robert N. Ford, "Job Enrichment Lessons from AT&T," *Harvard Business Review*, January-February 1973, p. 96.

11. Paul D. Greenberg and Edward M. Glaser, *Some Issues in Joint Union-Management Quality of Worklife Improvement Efforts* (Kalamazoo, MI: W. E. Upjohn Institute for Employment Research, 1980), p. 19.

12. Clayton Jones, "The Workers' Stake in Quality: A U.S. Idea Home to Roost," *The Christian Science Monitor*, September 25, 1981, p. 10.

13. Charles G. Burck, "What Happens When Workers Manager Themselves," *Fortune*, July 27, 1981, p. 64.

14. Irving Bluestone, "How to Put QWL to Work," unpublished paper presented to Work in America Institute, Washington, DC, December 6, 1979, pp. 7-8.

15. Judson Gooding, "It Pays to Wake Up the Blue-Collar Worker," *Fortune*, September 1970; also William A. Ruch and James C. Hershaver, "Productivity in People-Oriented Organizations," *Arizona Business*, May 1975, pp. 11-20.

16. Neal Q. Herrick, "The Other Side of the Coin," unpublished paper presented at the Twentieth Anniversay Invitational Seminar of the Profit Sharing Research Foundation, Evanston, IL, November 17, 1971.

17. John F. Witte, *Democracy, Authority, and Alienation in Work* (Chicago: University of Chicago Press, 1980).

18. Jeremy Main, "Westinghouse's Cultural Revolution," *Fortune,* June 15, 1981, pp. 74-93.

19. Robert H. Guest, "Quality of Worklife—Learning from Tarrytown," *Harvard Business Review,* July-August 1979, pp. 76-87.

20. David Jenkins, "Work Reform in France: A Ten-Year Record of Continuing Effort," *Jenkins Work Report,* February 1979 (supplement), pp. 17-24.

21. "Programme to 'Humanise' Workplace Comes Under Criticism," *The German Tribune,* May 9, 1980.

22. International Institute for Comparative Social Research, " 'Humanisation of Work' Between Labor Unions and the State—A Survey of Seven Countries" (West Berlin, West Germany: IICSR, 1980), p. 3.

23. John Logue, "On the Road Toward Worker-Run Companies? The Employee Participation Act in Practice," *Working Life in Sweden* (New York: Swedish Information Service, December 1978).

24. International Institute for Comparative Social Research, " 'Humanisation of Work' Between Labor Unions and the State—A Survey of Seven Countries," pp. 28-35.

25. Jack Barbash, "What Labor Wants Over the Next Decade," *Business Week* conference, Houston, TX, March 28, 1980, p. 7 (unpublished).

26. Glenn E. Watts cited in "The New Industrial Relations," *Business Week,* May 11, 1981, p. 86.

Chapter 8

1. J. Richard Hackman, "The Design of Work in the 1980s," *Organizational Dynamics,* Summer 1978, pp. 15-16.

2. R. E. Walton, "The Diffusion of New Work Structures: Explaining Why Successes Didn't Take," *Organizational Dynamics,* 1975 (No. 3), p. 21.

3. James O'Toole, "Thank God, It's Monday," *The Wilson Quarterly,* Winter 1980, pp. 130-131.

4. Louis E. Davis, "The Coming Crisis for Production Management: Technology and Organization," in Louis E. Davis and James C. Taylor, eds., *Design of Work* (Baltimore, MD: Penguin Books, 1972), p. 428.

5. Frederick Herzberg, "One More Time: How Do You Motivate Employees?" in *Ibid.,* p. 125.

6. Wickham Skinner, "The Impact of Changing Technology on the Working Environment," in Clark Kerr and Jerome M. Rosow, eds., *Work in America: The Decade Ahead* (New York: Van Nostrand Reinhold, 1979), p. 218.

7. Robert Schrank, "On Ending Worker Alienation: The Gaines Pet Food Plant," in *Humanizing the Workplace,* Roy P. Fairfield, ed. (Buffalo, NY: Prometheus Books, 1974), p. 129.

8. Paul D. Greenberg and Edward M. Glaser, *Some Issues in Joint Union-Management Quality of Worklife Improvement Efforts* (Kalamazoo, MI: W. E. Upjohn Institute for Employment Research, 1980), p. 21.

9. Irving Bluestone, "Worker Participation in Decision Making," in *Humanizing the Workplace,* pp. 53-54, 61.

10. "Where Being Nice to Workers Didn't Work," *Business Week* January 20, 1973, p. 98.

11. Jack Barbash, "Humanizing Work—A New Ideology," *The American Federationist,* July 1977, pp. 12-14.

12. Robert Schrank, *Ten Thousand Working Days* (Cambridge, MA: The MIT Press, 1978), p. 222.

13. John F. Witte, *Democracy, Authority, and Alienation in Work* (Chicago: University of Chicago Press, 1980), p. 2.

14. Davis, "Coming Crisis for Production Management," pp. 440-442.

15. George Strauss, "Is There a Blue-Collar Revolt Against Work?" in *Humanizing the Workplace,* p. 44.

16. "The New Industrial Relations," *Business Week,* May 11, 1980, pp. 96-98.

17. Mitchell Fein, "The Myth of Job Enrichment," in *Humanizing the Workplace,* pp. 76-77.

18. Peter S. Barth, "The New Mood in Labor-Management Relations," *The Wall Street Journal,* April 6, 1982; and A. H. Raskin, "The Cooperative Economy," *The New York Times,* February 14, 1982.

19. "Moderation's Chance to Survive," *Business Week,* April 19, 1982, p. 123.

20. Jack Barbash, "Reflections on Positive Collective Bargaining," *Labour and Society,* Vol. 6, January-March 1981, pp. 81-90.

21. Victor Gotbaum and Edward Handman, "Labor's Business," *The New York Times,* April 22, 1982.

Index